ROCK SOLID

ROCK SOLID

How to
Strengthen Your Company

JOHN CAMERON

iUniverse, Inc.
Bloomington

Rock Solid
How to Strengthen Your Company

iUniverse books may be ordered through booksellers or by contacting:

iUniverse
1663 Liberty Drive
Bloomington, IN 47403
www.iuniverse.com
1-800-Authors (1-800-288-4677)

ISBN: 978-1-4759-5419-7 (sc)
ISBN: 978-1-4759-5420-3 (hc)
ISBN: 978-1-4759-5421-0 (ebk)

Library of Congress Control Number: 2012920027

Printed in the United States of America

iUniverse rev. date: 11/05/2012

Author's Introduction

Rock Solid is a fable about strengthening companies. It's designed to be a how to book. Currently over six hundred thousand people in the United States alone go into business every year. To be successful, most of them need to learn how to build a strong company. On top of that there are literally millions of people already in business who wish their companies were rock solid and they're unsure about how to approach the challenge ahead of them. This book was written for them.

Strong companies consistently deliver great value to their customers, they attract good customers, they are profitable, they know their numbers better than most, they're very well organized, their employees are accountable and they easily take on new challenges.

You might think this sounds like utopia and I am inclined to agree with you. When you own a strong company life does get to be pretty good.

There's a question to ask yourself before you buy this book. Can *Rock Solid—How to Strengthen Your Company* deliver on its promise?

I know it can. I've seen it. As a business advisor and coach I have worked directly with hundreds of companies. I'm always amazed at how powerful the Five Key Elements of the Company Strength Program are. Time and time again they make significant, positive, lasting impacts on companies.

The book will introduce you to a fair amount of original content and several thought provoking new paradigms. The first is that, surprisingly, you do not own a business. What you actually own is

a company that does business in a market.

It's crucial for you to design a company that your target market wants to do business with. Why? It's because the people in the market own the business. Here's the proof: They can choose to give you their business and if your company doesn't meet or exceed their expectations they can take their business elsewhere. They can give it and they can take it away. That certainly sounds like the privilege of ownership to me.

Here's another interesting paradigm. When you own a company you should actually want problems. At first it's hard to believe, but it's true. The symptoms are really what you should be afraid of because they cause the most grief. The idea is to use the five key elements approach to systematically address the standard set of problems, typically encountered by owners as they build strong companies—before the symptoms start grinding away at you. The catch is that this approach requires some effort and it's often challenging to get around to the work when business is calling, but it's risky to put the work aside for too long. Ultimately it takes much less effort to build a strong company than it does to run one that's constantly suffering through symptoms.

This leads to an interesting observation. The business that individual companies are pursuing and processing is unique, much like individual people. This is in direct contrast to the set of problems that owners need to address as they strengthen their companies, which happen to be surprisingly similar.

Think about it this way. Entrepreneurs bring business ideas to life. Company owners build profitable organizations. As the business grows entrepreneurs need to make room for the company owner's mindset and get the work done. If they don't address the problems that are part and parcel of building a strong company then they're in danger of being caught up in an avalanche of symptoms. The avalanche can easily carry them down into the Valley of the Lost Entrepreneurs. This is not a great place to be. It's full of people working long hours for non-existent profits.

In the Valley people's lives are dominated by business. Their companies simply aren't strong enough to handle the business they're trying to process and the symptoms often spill over into their personal lives. This even applies when companies are starving for revenues. Specific strengths need to be developed in order to efficiently earn the business the company needs.

Rock Solid goes well beyond just identifying the problems. It drills into five key elements that effectively strengthen companies. The elements deliver proven solutions to the common problems. In fact, this book promises to have you working on the strength of your company even before you even finish reading it.

To make an analogy, a softball team needs to focus on the elements of throwing, catching, fielding, batting, and base running. If those elements are strong the team will be competitive during their games. If they're weak then there will be a variety of symptoms on display at every game they play.

The Five Key Elements of the Company Strength Program are listed below along with the page numbers indicating where they are introduced. There are also previews of them in the Prologue—which is a few pages ahead—then the fable clearly demonstrates how to implement them in your company. Reading the full story brings the elements to life and lets readers see them in action.

1   The AR²T of Momentum—page 19
2   Company Promise—page 40
3   Financial Information Systems—page 92
4   Company Accountability Matrix (CA³M)—page 133
5   BRIDGE Marketing Plan—page 181

It's also interesting to note that the softball elements need to be strengthened as the players reach new age levels. To be competitive a team of fifteen and sixteen year olds has to be stronger in the elements than a team of eleven and twelve year olds needs to be.

It's the same for companies. You might think that you won't be able to implement the full Company Strength Program, but the most successful way to approach is to choose one element and start there. Develop that element as much as you need to, and then select another one to work on. Keep going and before you know it you will have a strong company and good business will naturally follow. Continue working on the elements and business will be excellent.

This book isn't just for people stuck in the Valley of the Lost Entrepreneurs. It will benefit owners who already have their companies running reasonably well, particularly if there are expansion plans in the future. Introducing the Five Key Elements also helps with succession planning, which could involve passing the company on to your children or perhaps selling it to your employees. A strong company with the elements in place is clearly worth more when you're selling it on the open market. If you're retaining ownership of your company while retiring or stepping back from day to day operations, then this book will be extraordinarily useful.

There is a huge amount of talent stuck in the Valley of the Lost Entrepreneurs. The economy will improve significantly when these entrepreneurs build rock solid companies and return to being entrepreneurial again, especially with the advantages of their newly acquired knowledge, skills and financial resources. Jobs are created by entrepreneurs doing what they do best. Our economy was built one company at a time and it will be rebuilt one company at a time.

About twenty years ago I too was stuck in the Valley of the Lost Entrepreneurs. Sometimes I escaped on weekends and on the occasional holiday. I thank my wife Karen for that—she made me put the phone down and step away from the company. When I did escape, I searched many bookstores, several times, looking for a book that would show me how to build a strong company. I never found it. That's why I wrote *Rock Solid*.

The story involves an interesting cast of characters. There are, of course, the wise old veterans, but a fair amount is written from the perspective of Jen Russell, a recent university graduate. Jen and her friends represent the bright young people who are ready, willing, and able to help build the strength of the companies they work at.

This book is not about the impossible dream: it's about making the dream possible. It's written as an instruction manual for real people who are in business and want to build rock solid companies.

Please visit www.company-strength.com to get free downloads of the forms in the book.

Prologue

I looked at the clock in my car, it was 1:30. I'd just finished having lunch with Haley and Alice. All I had left to do was drop off a deposit for the hall and then I was free for the rest of the day. This was going to be the first clear Saturday afternoon that I had in months. I was looking forward to it.

My phone started to ring. I didn't recognize the number so I let the call go to my messages.

It was a beautiful day. Perhaps a nice walk by the river was in order.

My phone started to ring again. I checked the number; this time it was Dave. That was unusual. He didn't normally call me Saturdays so I answered it.

"Hello Dave, how are you doing?" I asked.

"I'm doing pretty well, how about you Jen?"

"Great, I've got the afternoon clear and I was just thinking about going for a walk."

"I've got a better idea. Why don't you come over to the batting cage? There's somebody here I'd like you to meet."

"I'm just leaving the Diamond Café now. I suppose that I can stop by for a few minutes," I replied.

"Thanks Jen, I appreciate it."

I stopped by the hall first to drop off the deposit and then I headed over to the batting cage.

As I walked into the entrance I saw Dave in the closest lane coaching one of the batters. He was offering her encouragement and feedback. I wasn't sure who was happier when she got a nice hit, Dave or her. After a minute or two he looked over my way. I waved to him and he waved back. Then he turned to the lane next to him and signalled the coach there to follow him to the door.

"Jen, I'd like you to meet Scott Borden. Scott, I'd like you to meet Jen Russell."

We exchanged greetings. Scott was clean cut. Even in his coaches' uniform he had a neat and tidy, business-like appearance. He appeared to be in his mid-forties. As we shook hands he looked at me and said, "So you're the one who won't take my calls."

Before I could respond, Dave cut in. "I'll get right to the point. Scott's told me that even though he loves coaching, he has to resign from the team because he's having some challenges at work. He owns Fort Pallet Management. It's a wood pallet management and manufacturing company. They expanded last year and set up a new operation over in Richmond. He tells me that both locations are having problems now and they aren't running very well. He's trying to figure out how to fix them and it's starting to take up a fair amount of his time. He doesn't think he'll be able to continue coaching ball."

I knew right then and there my free afternoon was gone.

"Jen, I told him that he's slipped into the Valley of the Lost Entrepreneurs and that you would show him the way out. I'll help him out with his softball team whenever he needs me to. Let's get him through this."

Out of the corner of my eye I could see that Scott was unsure. I'm about twenty years younger than him and I wasn't exactly dressed for work.

I figured that I should probably jump into the conversation. "Scott, let's head over to the Diamond Café. I'm pretty sure Dave can handle your team for rest of batting practice."

Dave smiled and nodded to me, shook Scott's hand, and started on his way back to the kids. Half way there he turned and called out, "Scott, I'll make sure your daughter Kaitlyn gets a ride home with one of the other players."

I drove over to the Diamond and arrived before Scott. The lunch rush was winding down and the Café was only three quarters full. I picked a booth at the front.

When he first sat down he looked me straight in the eyes and asked, "So, how do you plan to help me with my business?" There was a little attitude in his voice and it wasn't a good one.

"I know we're not getting off to a good start and I don't mean to be cheeky but, I don't think you actually own a business. What you really own is a company that does business in a market."

"Isn't that just semantics?" he asked. I could tell that he was skeptical.

"Not at all, it's an important distinction. Let me put it this way: it sounds to me like you were doing some good business and then you chose to expand. After that everything started to come apart at the seams. That's when you found out your company wasn't strong enough to handle that amount of business. Now you're not sure how to deal with it."

He looked at me and smiled for the first time. "That's actually pretty accurate. I haven't thought about that way before, but you're right."

"Can I tell you about a straightforward approach that's designed to strengthen your company?"

"Now you've got my attention," he said a bit more enthusiastically.

"It's called the Company Strength Program. It has five key elements. It does take some work to get them implemented, but after you've got them in place business will be good again."

The server came by and took our orders. We both asked for coffee. After she left I continued.

"In no particular order, the first element is the AR^2T of Momentum. Right now momentum appears to be taking your company in the wrong direction. This element will help you get that turned around. It's all about choosing the results you want and creating the momentum you need to get there. It's a dynamic four step process that's very good at finding solutions—even in challenging situations. It uses TRaction to bring the results to life. TRaction is short for Towards Results action. There's more to it than that, but once you learn how to manage your company's momentum its future looks a whole lot brighter.

That's a quick summary. For now I'm just going to give you the highlights of each element."

"That sounds good," he replied. I could tell that he was getting more interested.

"The next element is a Company Promise. It's all about the value you want your company to deliver to your customers. The main purpose of any company, anywhere, is to deliver value. Calling it a promise creates the right kind of focus for the people in your organization. Your value package should consist of both direct value and collateral value. We'll work through the process and get your company promise defined. After that we'll make sure it's up on everyone's radar so your company consistently delivers on it.

"Having a well thought out Company Promise typically raises the standards for the company and generally speaking the more value a company delivers—the more profit it makes. A strong company promise always connects well with a good business opportunity. If your promise doesn't match up with what the market is willing to pay for, then we've have even more work to do. Again, the full program gets into this in depth. This is the keystone element of the Company Strength Program. When you've got it right your whole organization is focused on delivering value that customers are willing to pay for."

"I've got a pretty good idea about what my company promise might be and I know it'll connect to a good business opportunity," Scott said. "I've always had good business growth. The problem is lately we haven't done a good job of delivering on it, as you say. I suppose that's partially because I haven't defined one yet."

"I'm pretty sure we can work through that," I said. "Let me tell you about the other three elements and then we'll figure out a good place to start."

The server came back to the booth with our coffees.

"Next comes Financial Information Systems. This element is all about managing and growing your company's profitability. It's based on a simple concept: if you get good information you'll make good choices and decisions and your company will be profitable. The primary purpose of accounting software packages is to process data into information, but all too often company owners only get trivia out of them. The difference is information helps you with your choices and decisions while trivia doesn't. We'll figure out what you need to know, when you need to know it, and design systems to get that information to you. You'll see Forecast and Variance Reports with Profit & Cost Centers, Key Performance Indicators, and some Balance Sheet Ratios, among other things."

"I have to confess, I don't really understand bookkeeping," said Scott, staring into his coffee.

"No problem. If you're like most company owners you have difficulty understanding your statements because the accounting rules were designed to serve the taxman, the bank, and investors in public companies. It's no wonder you don't understand them; they're not really about you. On the other hand, once we get good financial information systems in place you'll be in a much better position to manage and grow your profitability. You'll be operating your company like a professional." I replied.

"Business is a numbers game. I've got a friend named Alice. Dave and her are experts at this. They'll help us out here."

"I suppose I really should learn more about accounting, especially now with two locations. I can't be everywhere at once," said Scott.

"That leads me to the next element it will help you out with that as well. It's called the Company Accountability Matrix, or CA³M. It's a straightforward way to organize and systemize your entire company. It's extraordinarily useful, but it does take a while to wrap you mind around it at first."

"Let's hear it," he said.

"It starts out as a grid. Think about a spreadsheet. All of the functions the company performs over the course of a year are listed down the first column on the vertical axis. The people in your company are listed across the top row on the horizontal axis. Accountabilities, responsibilities, and communications are assigned by filling in the grid. Everything should be covered. It becomes a matrix when your company's systems, policies, job descriptions, and performance plans are drilled into it."

"That does sound a little complicated and we don't have systems or job descriptions and that kind of stuff."

"Don't worry, I'll help you get it all set up. I think the lack of systems might be a part of your problem," I said.

"That's a fair enough observation," Scott replied.

"People think systemizing a company is a challenging project, but the CA³M provides a roadmap that leads you through the process in an efficient manner. It's the only system for systemizing small companies that I've ever seen—which is interesting when you stop and think about it. Writing job descriptions and keeping them current is also pretty easy once you've built your CA³M."

"Scott, do you mind if I ask you a question?"

"No, go right ahead," he replied.

"Do you want your employees to be accountable and responsible?"

"That's a no brainer; of course I do," he answered a little tersely.

"Do you have a plan to make that happen?"

Scott looked at me and paused for a few seconds. "No, I don't," he said a little more softly.

"That's okay, not many owners do. The CA³M will address that for you as well. It takes some time to create your Company Accountability Matrix, but once you've got it built then you'll really be in position to get you company running like a finely tuned machine. It's a huge advantage."

"I'm pretty sure I could use that."

"I'll tell you about the last element," I said, "but it doesn't sound like you'll need it anytime soon. It's called the BRIDGE marketing plan. This element is all about getting the right customers for your company. The idea is to build a bridge between your company and the customers who can benefit from the value your company promise delivers.

"The BRIDGE acronym divides marketing up into six challenges, one for each letter. The first one is discovering the benefits your potential customers will buy into. The second challenge is, understanding your customers' resistance. If you have benefits they'll buy into and there's no resistance then you should get their business, but it's almost never that simple. The third challenge is initiating contact in a way that get's the right people's attention, in the right way. I said earlier that business is a numbers game, but marketing is a contact sport. I'm just motoring through the highlights here, but you'll find there's a lot more depth to the BRIDGE Marketing Plan when we drill into it."

"That's alright, keep going," he said.

"The fourth challenge is delivering some value along with your message. That way your prospects will stay engaged. The fifth challenge is getting feedback that you can use to improve. The sixth challenge is calculating your Return on Investment, or ROI."

"This Company Strength Program sounds pretty comprehensive."

"Once you get the hang of it, it becomes simple." I paused for a few seconds. "I'll draw a diagram for you."

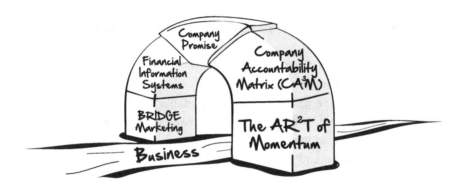

"The arch represents your company. It's a very strong shape especially when all of the five elements are rock solid. Then you can really flow a lot of business through it. What do you think Scott?"

"It looks like I should start working on at least four of the elements right away, but I've got to be honest with you though, my company is very tight on cash at the moment."

"I'm pretty sure Dave wants you to continue coaching softball. He's going to be helping you with your ball practices and you're going to learn a lot more than you expect to there. What it all boils down to is that I won't be sending you invoices any time soon. That doesn't mean that we won't be revisiting the deal at some point in the future, but for now all you have to do is keep coaching and I'll help you implement the Company Strength Program."

"That sounds too good to be true," Scott replied.

"You know, the other day I was out shopping for a wedding ring for my fiancé. I wound up buying an original, one of a kind ring because of something the jeweler said to me."

"What was that?"

"You have to take advantage of the opportunity of a lifetime during the lifetime of the opportunity. I don't know if you realize the scope of it yet, but what Dave is offering you is the opportunity of a lifetime and I think you're really going to enjoy it."

He picked up the diagram, rubbed his chin and looked out the window. I could almost hear him thinking. I didn't want to break his train of thought so I didn't say anything. After a minute he turned towards me.

"Okay, I guess I'm in, but there's one thing I want to know first. How did somebody as young as you figure all this out?"

"Well, it's a bit of a story. If you've got some time I'd be happy to tell you."

Scott checked his watch, looked back at me, and said, "I've got all afternoon."

PART ONE

Jen's Assignment

1

It all started with an assignment. I remember the day it was given to me. It was a Friday afternoon when I was called to Mr. Jones' office. That didn't happen very often. I was just a Junior Assistant at Carey Jones Norton. Mr. Jones was the lead partner and the head of the firm's tax department.

At first I thought that I was about to be let go. My job was to do whatever the accountants asked for. More and more I was just spending time trying to make myself look busy.

I couldn't help kicking myself again for taking a journalism degree. I enjoyed the studies but when I graduated the year before it turned out that there weren't many jobs available. I found work at a local coffee shop and continued to send out resumes to every company I could think of.

I was a bit surprised when Carey Jones Norton called me for an interview. All I really expected to get from it was a bit more experience being interviewed, but they seemed to like me and I was offered a junior assistant's job. The pay wasn't that great, but it seemed like a step up from the coffee shop and I figured I might be able make some contacts there that could eventually lead to a job that was more in line with my education.

That day as I headed towards Mr. Jones' office I thought, *it's back to being Jen Russell, the over educated barista working evening shifts, trying to pay off student loans, and survive in the city all by herself.* What kind of future was that? My prospects seemed pretty dim.

I walked slowly down the hall towards his office looking around and soaking it all in: the nice paintings on the walls, the fancy mouldings, and the offices with oak doors and big elegant desks. It was a good place to work. The people were friendly and treated me like a professional even though I was at the bottom of the company ladder. I felt good about working there.

Mr. Jones was different from the others. Not that he treated me badly; it was just that he didn't ever seem to acknowledge that I existed. He arrived early, left late, and always had his door closed. He only ever came out to meet his clients in the conference rooms and then he went straight back into his office. Everybody told me not to bother him unless it was absolutely necessary.

When I got down to his office I looked through the window next to his door and I saw him looking intently at his computer screen. I knocked gently as if not to disturb him, which is kind of funny when you think about it. "Come in," he said, a bit too sharply for my liking.

When I opened the door he asked, "Your name's Jen, isn't it?"

"Yes sir," I replied.

"Sit down. I'll be a couple of minutes," he said as he pointed to one of the leather wingback chairs across from his large cherry wood desk. It was the most impressive desk in the whole office. It matched the expansive bookcase that took up the entire wall behind him.

I sat down in the wingback chair and nervously looked around his office. It had large windows and a great view of the mountains. I couldn't help thinking that he probably never looked out at them. It seemed to be a bit of a waste for him to have the corner office, but I guess that's the way the corporate world works.

After a few minutes he looked up at me. "I hear that you're a writer. Is that right?" His question was direct and to the point.

"Well, I did do a lot of writing during my university days but not so much recently," I stammered. It wasn't the smartest thing to say. I figured that I should have paused for a second before I answered but my words were already out there.

"It's okay, I don't have anybody else." He didn't look or sound pleased. "I've got an assignment for you."

"Can you tell me more about it?" I asked. At this point I was relieved that I still had my job, yet somehow more nervous than ever. He looked out over his glasses. His glare seemed to cut right through me.

"Well, it's a bit of a story. Somebody's got me ticked off," he grumbled as he leaned back and folded his arms. "I was told that my firm didn't deliver any real value."

"Who would say such a thing?" I squeaked out. This conversation was making me feel really uncomfortable. I couldn't help but wonder what I was doing here and how I got caught up in this.

"It was Dave Ettinger from Velocity Software. He wasn't really trying to insult me but when he came in to discuss the tax planning for his exit strategy, he started to talk about how good his company had been to him, his family, his employees, his clients, to the community, and even to his suppliers. He

2

figures that it's getting near time to sell the company to his people and retire. I couldn't help myself. I started to tell him about Carey Jones Norton and how good it's been to me."

He leaned back again and ran his hand through his silver hair before continuing. "Dave doesn't see things the way I do. He was talking about having lots of time to spend with his family, the West Valley Softball League, and how Velocity Software really delivered value by helping business-people use technology to make their companies more competitive. He said Velocity was really dialed in on improving other peoples' companies.

"He even talked about the employees who passed through his organization and how their experiences at Velocity Software helped them make progress in their lives. He rambled on about a few ex-employees and how he was proud to help them achieve their personal ambitions, even when they didn't involve Velocity. He went on to say that the people he hired who really got what Velocity Software was all about were still there and the time for them to take over the company was fast approaching. He's getting ready to pass the torch."

"Sir, I don't get it. How is that different from the way you see things?" I said it before I could stop myself. *Oh crap,* I thought. *I just screwed up.* I could feel my face warming up and I think I went beet red as I sat there waiting for him to say something.

After what seemed like an eternity he responded. "Well, I always figured that business was about work. You work hard, put in long hours, and you'll be successful. Dave said that he learned a long time ago that business success comes from building strong companies that deliver value. He also said that he could see how that concept might have gotten lost in my business because our clients are legally required to do their taxes every year. If they don't they'll get into a lot of trouble. He agreed that I save them money by making sure that they don't pay any more than they have to. But then he said something interesting."

I was relieved that he didn't take offense to my previous question. I was getting curious about why I was here so I asked, "What was that?"

"He challenged me to think about a world that didn't have the tax thing, annual filings, or all of the other government regulations that I help my clients sort through. What would I do for them then? What value would I really like to deliver?

The way he views it is that lots of companies start every year. Most survive for a few years and some get firmly established and go on to be profitable. He thinks that we just wait for the survivors and then bill the crap out of them."

That was the first and only time that I've seen Mr. Jones smile and laugh, although there didn't seem to be any joy in it. "You know that meathead's got a point and it's been sticking in my craw for the past few months. That's where you come in."

How's that? I thought, but before I could ask he carried on.

"I'd like to deliver some value by helping people build and grow successful businesses. I'd like these businesses to add to the local economy and provide some good jobs for our young folks. It's probably the least I could do before I retire like Dave. I know that I don't really have the patience to work directly with the business owners myself, but I do have resources here at the firm. I should be able to coordinate this, given my experience."

It occurred me that I'd never been in business before and I was still wondering how I fit into this picture. Before I could say anything he started to talk again.

"Before you get going on this project I'd like to be clear on a couple of things. First off, it has to be rock solid. We have the reputation of the firm to protect here. I'd like you to write a whitepaper and it can't be just a bunch of platitudes. There's already way too much of that out there. It's got to have real substance."

Okay, I thought. *A whitepaper, I've written a couple of those before.* I raised my hand but he completely ignored me and continued on. I was getting the impression that he wasn't a very good listener.

"I searched the web and went down to the bookstore a few times where I spent a lot of hours looking at books. I even asked my clients about the books that they relied on while they were building their businesses. They gave me some ideas and there's some interesting stuff out there, but the book I wanted to read hasn't been written yet."

He didn't even ask me if I was interested or if I thought I could handle it. This was a lot to take in at once, especially since I hadn't expected it. I was trying to absorb what was happening as he went on.

"The second thing is that it has to be something a businessperson can pick up and start working with right away. I don't want people picking it up, reading it, and going, 'it all sounds good, but it won't work for me.' After they read our whitepaper they should know what to do next."

Finally I got a chance to speak. "Why did you pick me for this project?" I asked. "I don't have any business experience at all."

"That's exactly it. I tried to do this myself, but what I found is the project started to get too complex. It isn't as easy as I thought it was going to be. There are way too many ideas flying around in my head and they just aren't coming together the way I want them to. I'm thinking that it might take somebody with no preconceived notions about business to write this. To be successful it has to make sense and it has to be easy to read. I just can't seem to get there myself."

I wasn't sure that I followed his logic but I liked the idea of putting my degree to use so I agreed to take on the project.

"When I read the resume you sent in a few months ago, I told them to hire you. I suspected that this point in time was coming." He leaned back in his chair again. Mr. Jones was a large and imposing man.

"There's a quotation I came across by Oliver Wendell Holmes that I'd like you to think about as you write," he said as he pointed over to a box of books and files in the corner. "That's a good place to start. If you can make the stuff inside the box work with the quotation on the top, then I'll know that you hit the mark."

Then the meeting was over. "I've got to get back to work now," he said as he turned back to his computer screen. I walked over to the box and read the quotation written on the lid.

I would not give a fig for simplicity this side of complexity,
but I would give my life for simplicity on the other side of complexity.
Oliver Wendell Holmes

2

That meeting was a couple of months previous. Earlier in the day I'd told Alice, the receptionist at Carey Jones Norton that I was heading out to do some more research. In reality I just couldn't sit at my desk staring at a blank computer screen any longer. My fingers were poised and ready to type but my brain couldn't come up with anything worthwhile.

I'd read everything in the box Mr. Jones gave me, talked to everybody in the office, and interviewed dozens of the firm's clients. I also enlisted ten of Carey Jones Norton's clients to participate in the project. They agreed to try out some of the concepts that were being considered for the whitepaper. Afterwards I'd visit regularly and observe how their companies were developing. They were my test clients. Mr. Jones wanted the concepts had to be rock solid and ready to implement and I wanted to make sure they passed the test.

Every time I thought I was making some headway the ideas were either too simple to make it through the field of complexity intact or the ideas got completely lost in there.

I was starting to believe that building a company was just too complex a project to make simple. Even seemingly solid advice like developing a business plan had trouble in the real world. Not many companies had them and when I asked owners whose companies were doing well why they didn't have business plans, they said they didn't need them. They believed that it was more important to be flexible and adapt quickly. To them, business was about being nimble and reacting to changing circumstances.

Others said to focus on the customers. The next moment someone else was saying it's all about your people. Lots of people said it was cashflow, cashflow, cashflow, but then one of the accountants explained the Net Trade Cycle to me and said that with a positive Net Trade Cycle cashflow can be good even when a company isn't profitable. I heard that the key is developing systems so average people can be effective and next I heard that having good people is the key. I was finding out that there were many contradictions in business advice.

I hoped a drive and a change of scenery would somehow help me make sense of it all.

Having passion was a common theme in the literature but it appears to me that it's been driven out of most owners. I tried telling a couple of my clients that they needed more passion. They just laughed at me.

Leadership is another good one. There are so many books out there that it makes your head spin. They all sound great when you read them but I got blank stares when I recommend the ideas. I could almost hear people thinking that I had no idea what business was all about.

Half of my clients stopped taking my calls. One even told me that I needed to work in a real business to find out what it was like. He didn't think I had any idea what I was talking about.

After I left the office I was lost in thought, driving aimlessly in my old Honda Civic, when it seemed to shift into autopilot and head towards the old coffee shop I used to work at. I smiled and shook my head. It probably knew I'd be working back there soon enough. I may as well stop in and say hello.

"Hey, how's it going, Haley?" I called out as I opened the door and took a deep breath. I loved the smell of freshly ground coffee and it was good to connect with an old friend from more easygoing days. I'd worked quite a few shifts with her and I always enjoyed her company. The place still looked the same, just like the other coffee shops on almost every corner nowadays.

"Hey you," she replied. "We were just talking about you the other day."

"Really? Only good stuff I hope."

"Of course! We were wondering why you haven't been around for a while. Things must be going well over at the accounting office. How is it going, by the way?"

"Well, not so good lately. Can you pour me a cup of the Morning Brew?"

"Sure, not a problem, for you anything!" She poured the coffee and laughed. "I thought I'd try one of your own funny little sayings on you. That's what we were talking about: you always seemed to have a way with words. Hey, it's almost time for my break. Do you mind if I grab a cup and join you?"

I scanned the place for an empty table. "I'd like that. I'll get us the table in the corner over there."

Haley listened remarkably well as I went over the whole story in detail. Right down to my renewed fears that I was about to be let go. Mr. Jones didn't seem to like much of what I'd written up to that point. He was even more grumpy than usual lately and I really didn't like interrupting him. It was never a pleasant experience.

I wasn't all that impressed with what I'd assembled either. I wondered aloud whether or not the project was even possible.

"If I ever meet that Dave Ettinger who pissed off Mr. Jones and set this whole thing in motion, I'll give him a piece of my mind."

"Dave Ettinger? Really, he's the one that got your boss ticked off? You're not talking about the softball coach are you?"

Uh-oh, I thought. *Here we go again.* Somehow I put my foot in my mouth for what seemed to be the thousandth time this month. This project has to be cursed. I couldn't believe that it was happening again. "I've never met him, all I know about him is that he owns Velocity Software," I sighed.

"Yup, that's him." She smiled. "I didn't think he ever ticked anybody off."

"You know him?" I still couldn't believe my bad luck. Haley seemed to like him too, which made it even worse. I looked down at the table and rubbed my forehead.

"Sure," she said. "And you know what, if he got you into this mess the chances are good that he'll help you get out of it. He's like that. I'll be seeing him tonight. We've got a slow pitch game in West Valley and his team practices on the next field over. Do you want me to talk to him for you?"

At that point I didn't think that I had anything to lose, so I agreed. We caught up on the local gossip as we finished our coffees and then I headed back to work.

3

The next morning I got my coffee and settled into my desk. The phone rang as I was turning on the computer expecting to stare blankly at the screen again.

"Hello Jen, this is Stan Bolman from Velocity Software. Dave Ettinger asked me to give you a call and see if you were available to come by this afternoon at three."

"Sure," I said, thinking that I could get the address from our files. I was surprised how quickly the president of a company like Velocity Software responded to me. There was no money involved and most business owners I spoke to recently thought I was just wasting their time.

"When Dave told me to schedule you in I asked him what it was about and he said that you were in a bit of a pickle. I think it was about writing a whitepaper for company owners. He was saying that he wanted to understand something about a field of complexity. Do you mind if I ask you what it's about?"

"It's about to drive me nuts, that's what it's about," I replied.

"Well try and describe it to me," Stan responded cheerfully. "Maybe it'll help."

I thought for a couple of seconds and started to talk. "When you ask owners who've built great companies what the keys to success are, they all have opinions based on their own experience. They sound good at the time but when you take most of those ideas back to people who are just grinding it out, they'll tell you why it won't work in their situation or that they already knew that," I hesitated. "It just isn't what they need right now. Something that survives the field of complexity has to work well at both ends of the spectrum." As I was talking I started to realize that I was actually making some sense for a change. "The ideas have to be able to work for business people who haven't gotten their companies firing on all cylinders yet. Companies aren't built overnight and the journey to rock solid is a lot more challenging than most people expect."

"Hmm, that seems interesting," Stan said. "I can see why Dave wants to talk to you. It seems like a valuable project and he's always helping people out. He gets a real kick out of seeing folks achieve their goals. Just a thought though: your audience for this paper appears to be pretty broad. Are you writing this for people who are just starting out or for people who've got a company up and running and want to grow the business some more?"

"I'm not sure; I haven't really thought about that before. It's a good question," I said.

I took the rest of the day to try and assemble my thoughts so I wouldn't appear to be completely lost when I met with Dave Ettinger. I only had an hour with him. I normally started work at 8:00 AM and my regular day mercifully ended at 4:00 PM.

I looked through the box that Mr. Jones had given me. It was now overflowing. Then I reviewed the notes I'd taken about my clients and decided to focus the project on the size of the five companies that would still talk to me. They ranged from four to twelve employees with revenues of $350,000 to just over $1,200,000.

That seemed to narrow it down to a reasonable project. What rock solid strategies could be readily implemented in a company that size that would move them to that mystical next level everyone kept mentioning? A lot of people talked about moving their business to the next level.

I laughed at how naïve I was at the start of this project. I figured I could just ask people what the next level was and from there all I would have to do is show it to successful business-people and they would be able to tell me what it took to get there.

I arrived at Velocity Software at 2:50 and asked for Stan. I was hoping he'd be there to introduce me to Mr. Ettinger.

Stan emerged from the back and brought me down to Mr. Ettinger's office. On the way he told me to make sure to call him Dave. Apparently Dave had a way of treating everyone as an equal, no matter who they were.

As we walked into his office he got up from behind his old oak desk. Dave was very friendly, like he was greeting a guest in his house. He thanked Stan and asked me if I wanted a coffee, water, or anything else. I politely declined. He casually motioned his hand towards a small round table in the corner with two chairs. It wasn't all that impressive of an office. It was well used and you could tell that he'd been working in it for years. The walls were covered in pictures. Both of his bookcases were packed full of books and mementos.

The first thing he did after we sat down was apologize to me. "I'm sorry, Jen. Haley told me that I punched Al Jones' buttons a few months back and it kind of exploded on you. I didn't mean for that to happen. She tells me you've been given a project that's driving you crazy."

"You don't need to apologize," I said. "I think that maybe I'm getting a handle on it now."

"Excellent, I'd like to hear more about it. When Haley described it to me it sounded like a challenging assignment. I rolled it around in my head last night and it's been on my mind all day. That's why I asked for a three o'clock meeting. I wanted to take some more time to think about it before we met."

I could instantly tell why people liked him. He made me feel important and he was genuinely interested in what I had to say. Plus he was happy I was making progress. Dave hardly knew me, but somehow I could sense that he cared about me.

"Why don't you start by telling me how you're approaching it?" he asked gently.

I told him I'd decided to ask successful business owners to tell me their stories about how they reached the next level when they were in the $350,000 to $1,200,000 range. Then I'd look for commonalities. From there I'd draft a report and take it back to my clients. I made quotation marks with my fingers as I said the word 'clients'. "After that I'm going to check back every week or so and see what they're implementing. As their companies move forward I'll know what's rock solid."

"That's brilliant," he said. "I think you're on the right track although I think you'll find that the next level means something different to everyone. You'll likely have to do some work clarifying what it means for the purpose of your assignment."

"Yeah, you're right. The way people talk about the next level almost makes it seem like a mythical place where everything is better." I started mentally going through my clients thinking about what the next level meant to them and I really couldn't come up with anything in common other than more revenues. Thankfully Dave interrupted my train of thought.

4

"Jen, I'd like to volunteer to be one of your successful company owners, if you'll have me. I think you'll find the story about Velocity Software at that size to be very interesting. It was twenty years ago, but I remember it like it was yesterday."

I quickly agreed. I hadn't felt this good for weeks. It seemed like the weight of the world was lifting off of my shoulders. As I took a moment and smiled I noticed that he was writing three words on a piece of paper:

Zone

Decide

AR^2T

"What's that all about?" I asked.

"They're three words that I learned from an old friend, but before we get to them I'd like to talk about this field of complexity thing that Haley mentioned. It's really piqued my interest and I'm trying to wrap my mind around it. It has something to do with an Oliver Wendell Holmes quotation, doesn't it?"

"Yes it does. Mr. Jones taped the quotation to the top of a box of materials he gave me. It's:

I would not give a fig for simplicity this side of complexity,
but I would give my life for simplicity on the other side of complexity."

"Well, let's make a trade: I'll tell about these three words," Dave said as he tapped his fingers on the paper in front of him, "if you'll tell me what you think Holmes meant by his quotation."

It was a simple request. I should have been able to answer it easily but my mind went blank. This wasn't good. How could I get this far into the project without understanding this? I had to say something and I was faced with making it up as I went. I took a deep breath.

"I suppose he was struggling with a difficult problem and he wanted to devise a method of solving it easily. Something he could replicate on future occasions. I think that he recognized that sometimes simplicity finds the best solutions and other times it leads nowhere. He certainly saw that some simplicity can be of great value while other simplicity is of no value at all. It's often difficult to tell the difference."

I paused and Dave interjected. "That's what I was thinking too. I found it interesting that he didn't mention making the problem less complex."

I quickly jumped back in. "That's it. It's the simplicity that helps to navigate a complex challenge that he would give his life for."

"I see what you mean," he replied. "I was puzzled by his references to 'this side' and 'the other side' for a while. It was like the complexity and simplicity weren't in the same place at the same time but I agree with you: I think the simplicity he prefers helps people move through complexity."

I surprised myself with the clarity I suddenly felt. "They have to coexist! The simplicity that he wouldn't give a fig for gets chewed up and spit out by complexity. The simplicity he'd give his life for navigates the field of complexity and gets to the other side. It makes the journey easier."

"That's the way I'm starting to understand it too," Dave replied. "I can see why Jones thinks the quotation applies to business. Building a strong company is a complex project with a surprising amount of moving parts. A whitepaper that helped owners navigate through it would be extremely valuable.

"That brings something else to mind. Simplicity on the other side of complexity likely has some substance to it. I think that it's fair to assume that simplicity on the other side includes a good understanding of the complexity in the environment. I imagine once you get to the other side you'll know a lot more about what you didn't know when you first got started. There has to be some learning involved and sometimes the hardest part is figuring out what it you need to learn. It can be right in front of you and hard to see at the same time. I can really identify with that. I've been there."

Dave leaned back in his chair, took a brief moment to collect his thoughts, before he continued. "I think it's important to create a clear distinction between the business and the company. Most people think they own a business, but they actually own a company that does business in a market. The company is the entity; business is what the company does and the market is who it does it with."

"I've never thought of it that way before," I said.

He went on. "You know, sometimes people use the word business to describe a market opportunity. They say things like: 'I'd like to get into the construction business,' or, 'IT is a good business to be in right now.' Other times they use it to describe the activity. They say things like: 'I'm doing business with so and so,' or, 'It's good doing business with you.' Still other times they use it to describe a company. They say things like: 'Microsoft is a good business,' or, 'Apple is a good business.' The word business gets used in a lot of different ways."

"Why is that important?" I asked.

"Well, if you use the word loosely and somebody tells you to work on your business, what are you going to do? That type of confusion just adds to the complexity. When you're learning about a complex environment it really helps when you can see all of the pieces of the puzzle clearly. That makes the challenge more straightforward.

"When Velocity was at the size you're talking about I kept growing the business without strengthening the company and I almost wound up losing the whole shooting match. It got to the point where the company just wasn't strong enough to handle the business we were doing."

"Now that's interesting," I said as I wrote in large letters in my notepad.

A company does business in a market

"I was like a lot of people in business: I was interested in the market and I knew the business, but I didn't understand how to build a strong company to support it. To make matters more complex, like a lot of owners I had my company doing business in more than one market. I was lucky enough to run into somebody who helped me navigate Velocity through it."

"I'd like to know more about that."

"His name is Mark McKinley and you'll hear plenty about him as I tell you the story about Velocity at that size. Mark focused on five key elements. He also coached softball and used the same approach there. His softball elements were throwing, catching, fielding, batting, and base running. When a team is strong in all five they'll be competitive when they play their games."

"His Five Key Elements for company strength are: The AR^{2}T of Momentum, Company Promises, Financial Information Systems, Company Accountability

Matrixes (CA³M), and BRIDGE Marketing Plans. He had his ways of strengthening them all. When a company is strong in all five key elements it will do a lot of good business."

"Now that's interesting. I'd like to learn more about them," I said.

"No problem but, first I need to keep my end of the bargain we made a few minutes ago and tell you about these three words," he said as he pointed to the piece of paper on the table in front of him.

We started with Zone. He asked me to draw a four inch circle in the middle of a page and another larger six inch circle around that. Inside the middle circle he asked me to write Comfort Zone. In the space between the two circles he asked me to write Learning Zone. Then he asked me to write Panic Zone outside of that.

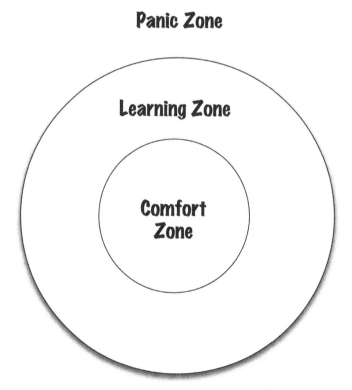

"I just want you to know that I think you're a pretty smart person," he said. "I suspect the reason that you've been having so much trouble with this project is that Jones threw you right into the panic zone. You've got a journalism skill set that's in your comfort zone, but not much in the way of direct experience with the subject matter. That appears to be where the challenge is. Everyone's learning zone has a boundary and that's represented by the perimeter of the second circle. Beyond that it's hard to make progress and it gets frustrating, but I guess you know that already."

Dave glanced directly at me. I smiled back.

"A good coach or mentor can expand your learning zone and help you get through it more efficiently," he said. "Having a roadmap, drawn with input from people who've gone before you, works very well too. I think that's what your whitepaper will be for company owners."

That's a great way of putting it, I thought.

"I don't think you've been given enough support and guidance to get the end result that Jones wants. That doesn't mean you're not capable of delivering. It appears to me that you're headed in the right direction and the more effectively you use your time in the learning zone the bigger your comfort zone will get."

A wave of relief washed over me. I started to relax. Dave was making me feel confident and he seemed to understand what I was going through.

"If I was in your place it would be hard not to be upset with Jones, but on the other hand I think there's some merit in giving this project to someone like you with no business experience. Too many people in the business world are too attached to their own ideas. Somebody like you should be able to come up with objective opinions. You can let concepts survive or fail on their own merit."

"Thanks, Dave. I really appreciate your help."

"No problem. You know, at the stage you're talking about most owners are in their comfort zone when it comes to doing business, but they're in their learning zones or their panic zones when it comes to strengthening their companies. They don't move forward; sometimes because they just don't know how to. I know it seems strange, but it's not that uncommon for business-people to think they should somehow know everything already, just because they own a company. Many owners also have difficulty admitting to what they don't know. Typically they like to be seen as being in control of every situation. This makes it hard for them to ask for help or even to get another opinion. I was guilty of that for far too long."

"I have a hard time seeing that," I said.

Dave looked over and smiled.

"Having a mentor and a clear roadmap to follow is a big advantage. Mark and his five key elements provided that for me at that stage of growth. His elements still ring true today. I'll point each of them out as I tell the story. You'll see that they combine to become the Company Strength Program."

Next we moved on to decide. He asked me to write the word at the top of another page. Then he asked me to write homicide, genocide, suicide, and pesticide below that.

Decide

Homicide

Genocide

Suicide

Pesticide

"See anything?" he said, smiling.

I laughed. "Sure. They all have the same root word. From the looks of things it means to kill off. I've never noticed that before."

"That's why I like making choices instead of decisions," Dave said. "Some people think it's a pretty thin distinction." He chuckled. "I admit they're both ways of narrowing things down and making a selection, but in my mind choices are much more powerful. They clearly identify the results you really want. Decisions, on the other hand, are arrived at by the process of elimination and sometimes they kill off the results you'd actually prefer."

"Can you be a little clearer about that?" I asked.

"Sure. Choices are about going after what you want. Choices often require shifting into the learning zone. They are harder to make than decisions, but over time consistently making choices has a huge positive impact.

"For example: a company owner might choose to be in the mid to high end of the market where the margins are better. When you choose to be there it follows that you have to offer premium products and service. You'll have to be consistent with your pricing. Both you and your staff will need to be able to respond effectively when customers ask for discounts. The overall standards for your operation will have to be higher than your competitors. Your employee training will likely be more involved. Your skills as a manager will be tested and even your company's marketing will be more challenging.

"It's tougher to make a choice like this. It's easier to kill off the choice and decide to go for the mid to low end of the market because of any one of a hundred excuses. This happens way more often than you think.

"Far too often people make decisions, whether they know it or not, just to stay in their comfort zones. That can kill off the outcomes they really want.

"Am I making sense here?" I nodded and he continued.

"So, did you make a choice or a decision when you narrowed the project?" He grinned.

I was finding out that Dave liked to make people think. It was a great question.

"Well, it'll be easier to move forward," I said. "And it'll be great to make some progress for a change, but I suppose that it won't test the whole field of complexity anymore. It'll just take into account a part of the journey that a company owner makes."

"Is that a choice you want to make?" he asked.

At that point I laughed. We had a great chat for the next few minutes. By the end of it we'd reached the conclusion that the size of business I'd chosen for my whitepaper was an important part of the field on almost every company owner's journey. A few would choose to stay smaller than this for personal reasons but most wanted to at least reach this size and beyond. It was logical that the answers I sought had to work well here. Later on I could check to see how they worked in larger and smaller sized companies.

We both agreed that when this project was completed it would be capable of delivering a substantial amount of value to a lot of people. It didn't make sense to make decisions that limited the potential value. It did make sense to choose to narrow the focus for the time being because it would put me in the learning zone instead of the panic zone. It was like dividing the project into phases.

5

My journalism training kicked in. "So tell me about the choices you've made," I said.

Dave's face broke into a big smile. "No problem, I'll get to them as the story unfolds. It'll be much more interesting to see them in the context of Velocity's development. Don't worry, I'm coming to that, but here's one other thing first. We haven't talked about the last word on the page yet and it's a pretty important word to me. It's one thing to make choices, but it's something else altogether to have a process to make them happen."

"This sounds like it could be very useful," I said.

"I know it is. After I explain it to you I'll tell you the story of how Velocity Software survived the stage you're interested in. You'll be able to see how and why I made the choices I did. It was a tough stage and believe me it was touch and go for a while. I almost lost the company back then."

Art was the next word. As I looked at the page in front of him I could see that he wrote it in

capital letters. There was a small two over the R like it was a number to be squared: AR^2T.

"This is one of Mark's five key elements for company strength," Dave said. "The full name for it is the AR^2T of Momentum. This is a process that effectively turns choices into realities. It creates the kind of momentum you really want your company to have. We use it regularly here at Velocity Software and it's helped us build a strong company. It takes a few minutes to describe it, so stay with me here."

He wrote an **A** in the top left corner of a fresh sheet of paper with an **R** three inches below that, another **R** three inches below that, and a **T** three inches below that.

"I think that part of the reason your project appears to be so difficult is because business is as much an art as it is a science. In science there is one right answer, but with art, beauty is in the eye of the beholder." He leaned back and rubbed his chin before he continued. "Strengthening a company leans more to the scientific side. The type of business it processes is more on the artistic side.

"When it comes to doing business, not everyone has to make the same choices to be successful. Owners have to make the choices that are right for themselves and their companies. Microsoft and Apple made different choices, for example. Both companies started at about the same time, in the same industry and they went on to become two of the most valuable companies in the world, but they made completely different choices along the way."

Dave smiled and ran his hand through his hair.

"This is where the magic comes in." He started writing on the page again. When he turned it around to face me it read:

Assessment

Realize the Results you want

Realize your options

TRaction

"It all starts with **Assessment**. You need an accurate picture of where you're at. This can be difficult for owners to do by themselves. In a lot of situations you think you can, but it always works better when other people are involved. Sometimes you don't even know what questions to ask yourself. This is particularly true when a person is doing something for the first time. Most company owners are first timers. Only a small percentage of people go on to develop a second company and even less start a third. On top of that, every stage of growth brings new challenges and that puts owners back into the learning zone. If you haven't built a company before it can be very difficult to know what pieces of the puzzle you might be missing. Fairly often the problem that's holding a company back is a missing piece or two. Building a strong company is a big and challenging project. It actually surprises me how few owners get periodic assessments along the way. There's a lot at stake.

"It doesn't have to be expensive. There are industry associations and business groups that could develop something like this. You can even get it done through your personal network if you have an assessment process in place."

Dave stopped talking and looked around his office. His eyes settled on a picture of a softball game and he seemed to drift off.

"Are you okay?" I asked.

"There's an old saying: 'what you don't know can't hurt you,' but in business what you don't know can kill your company or at least make your life a lot more difficult. On the other side of the coin, learning the right things makes the journey much easier."

He looked back towards the picture again.

"I'm just remembering back to when I learned this. It was twenty years ago but I remember it clearly. I almost gave up on Velocity." He paused and turned back towards me. "I've got to tell you about the rest of the AR²T of Momentum before I start telling the story or I might sound like an old man rambling on."

He took another look at the picture before continuing.

"The **R** is squared because there are two of them. The first one stands for **Realize the Results you want**. This is where you look out the windshield and see where you want to go. You're in the driver's seat and you're in charge of making the choices for the company. A company owner could choose to increase their margins, start a new product line, make their operation more efficient, increase their profits, or grow their revenues, for example. The beauty of the AR²T of momentum is that you can make choices even if you don't know how to get there yet. The next two steps bring your choices to life.

"This brings us to the second **R,** which is **Realize the Options.** Here the objective is to figure out what options you have to close the gap between where you are and where you want to get to. It's important to get as many ideas as possible. The key is not to use critical thinking. This step is a creative process. If somebody's got an idea, add it to the list with no questions asked. A very successful friend of mine has a saying: 'I've got a lot of great ideas and some of them actually work.' That's the right attitude here.

"It's always good to have an inventory of options to choose from. They bounce off of each other and create new ones. If you and your people are short on ideas, then ask yourselves, 'if we don't know the answer, then who do we know that might?' Then go ask them. Another interesting question is, 'if we already knew how to get that result, what would we know?' That puts a different spin on things and it can often lead to interesting solutions."

"Those are great questions," I said.

"Over the years I've gotten a lot of good ideas from using them," he replied casually.

"So, if you've taken the time to work through the AR²T of momentum you know where you're at, you've chosen the results you want, and you've got an inventory of options for getting there. That's still not enough."

"The **T** stands for traction. When you write it use a capital **T** followed by a capital **R** then **action**. In short form it's **TRaction**. In long form it reads **T**owards **R**esults **action**. This is the step that's often missing. A lack of follow through is a common theme in small companies. It's easy to get busy with the business and put company strengthening initiatives on the back burner. I sure suffered from that before I met Mark, but ever since then I've always made them a priority and it's made a huge difference in the development of my company."

Dave stopped and drew four large boxes on the page below each of the letters.

"The concept is to review the inventory of ideas that you've got in the realize the options box and put them into a logical sequence. Sometimes the options gel into a strategy, but it's more important that they get converted into tasks with deadlines. These items get moved on to the TRaction plan for the week. As the previous week's TRaction plan is completed, a new TRaction plan is created with the next items from the inventory. As you take action, fresh new ideas emerge. Delegation is also an important skill at this point. The AR²T of momentum works better when there is teamwork and regular meetings involved. I know from personal experience that this approach can take on large challenges and deliver impressive results."

"That's a neat process," I commented.

"As you gain TRaction, you'll also get feedback and make adjustments to your inventory of options. It's a dynamic process that can take weeks or months to unfold, depending on how challenging the choice is."

"Alright, I'm ready to tell you the story of Velocity Software at that stage now. You'll see the AR²T of momentum come to life. It's one of Mark's five key elements and I wanted you to know about it in advance because it plays an important role in the story."

"Thanks," I said as I looked down at my notes again.

"There's only one place to start and that's right at the beginning," Dave said as he settled back into his chair and launched into the story.

PART TWO

Dave Tells Velocity's Story

6

I'll never forget the day things started to turn around. It was so improbable, so unexpected, and yet it seemed completely natural at the same time. The transformation didn't happen immediately. It was a lot of hard work in the weeks and months that followed but there is no denying that everything began to change for the better that day in West Valley Park.

I'd taken my daughter Ann to her softball practice and settled on to the metal bleachers down the third base line. I purposely selected the farthest spot so I could sit there undisturbed. I was hoping the other parents dropping off their kids wouldn't notice me there and want to chat. I didn't feel like talking to anyone. It seemed that I felt that way more and more lately. It took me a while to get comfortable on those bleachers. I leaned as far back as possible, hands behind my head, and was soon lost in thought.

I can't remember exactly what I was thinking about but I'm pretty sure I was worrying about my business problems. That seemed to be my favorite hobby back in those days. Velocity was struggling and I wasn't sure that it was going to survive. I just couldn't get it off my mind. I was constantly worried that my company was going to fail. I figured that I'd pretty much destroyed my life and I'd have to start all over again. My business worries had taken over my life. I was drowning in them.

A few years before that, the start of softball season was one of my favorite times of year. The warmth of the spring sun, the smell of the freshly cut grass, the chatter of kids playing ball; I loved it. I used to coach my daughter's teams and I enjoyed getting to know the players and their families. As a dad, it was one of those great experiences I got to share with Ann.

Unfortunately, coaching softball had fallen by the wayside like almost everything else I enjoyed about life. I'd bought into the idea that building the business involved hard work and long hours. I kept it up for a long time, but there on those bleachers I was out of gas. I couldn't see how I could work any harder and the business was consuming all of my time as it was.

The day things started to get better, you see, began as one of the worst days of my life.

That morning I'd met with the bank. My company, Velocity Software, was hanging on by a thread. It wasn't pretty. A few years before I was playing with some program code on my computer when I had an idea for enterprise resource planning software that any small manufacturer could use. It was brilliant and so simple. I knew I could do this thing. I told my wife it was a million dollar idea and it would level the playing field for small manufacturers who have to compete against larger companies and foreign importers.

"Then let's do it," she said.

So I did, or at least I tried. I quit my job, cashed in some investments, set up the company, rented some office space, bought some computers, and hired a software programmer to help me. Day and night for ten months we worked on the software, building the product from scratch. It was exhilarating and excruciating at the same time. Every night I went to bed thinking that this was the best working experience I had ever been a part of.

When I was sitting on those uncomfortable bleachers in the park that day, my initial excitement was a long way off. The company was now going nowhere fast. Every month my wife Karen and I got further behind. We were personally maxed out on a few credit cards just trying to stay afloat. My staff, now eight people, was edgy and concerned. They could see that we were struggling to pay the bills and they knew we were shaky. Morale had plunged. The mornings were the worst for me. I didn't know if I could face another drive to work. I kept thinking about the eight employees and their families, so dependent on the company for their wages. My wife and I were exhausted at the prospect of more debt. We fought almost every night after the kids went to bed. I didn't think I could go on.

I feel guilty even saying this but the appointment with my banker had filled me with grim resolve. Driving to the bank that morning, I was secretly hoping that he would pull the plug on the whole thing. There was simply no way we were going to make it and the bank wasn't going to throw good money after bad. They'll kill it today, I thought, and then I'll be free.

But my bank officer didn't do it. He just wouldn't put me out of my misery. "It's a good product," he said. "You need to give it a chance." I know that he was just repeating what I said to him at our previous meetings back when I was full of enthusiasm, but now when I heard him talking about the bright future for the software—I was having trouble believing it. He must have thought that he was helping when he extended my loan and found a few more thousand to put in and keep us alive. It was hopeless, but he didn't see it. Maybe he thought I wanted to keep going. I didn't know that for sure but I did figure this new money would be gone by next quarter. I was captaining the Titanic, and there was only one way this thing was going to end.

As these dark thoughts swirled around me, my eyes fell on a large banner on the scoreboard in centerfield. It read, 'West Valley Softball League, Where Everybody Wins.' Everybody wins? What about me? I'm not winning.

Ping!

"Heads up! HEADS UP!"

BANG!

A foul ball blasted off Ann's aluminum bat and ricocheted into the bleachers right next to me. If I hadn't known better I would've thought she was trying to kill me. Ann ran over to the fence.

"Geez, Dad, you didn't even flinch!" she said incredulously.

"No fear," I smiled weakly.

Ann's coach, Mark, wandered over to the fence in front of me.

"You all right?" he asked.

"Just a close call," I replied.

Mark looked me in the eyes for just a second. He seemed to read my mind.

"Okay, girls, head to the outfield for fly balls," he called out. He turned to his assistant coach. "Phil, can you handle them for a few minutes?" Phil nodded as he picked up a bat and a bucket of balls. Mark walked through the gate and sat down next to me.

"It's Dave, right?" he asked. "You run a software company, don't you?"

"Yeah," I said, impressed that he remembered my name from one brief introduction at parents' night three weeks earlier. Must be his business training, I thought, recalling the business card he handed out that night. All it said on it was his name, phone number, and that he was a Softball Coach and Business Advisor.

"You okay?" he asked. "You look like you have the weight of the world on your shoulders."

"Bad day at the office," I replied.

"Want to talk about it?"

I hesitated. It was funny timing. I'd been thinking about asking Mark for advice since I left the bank that morning. I didn't even know him, but I knew I could use some kind of help and Ann seemed to like him. All afternoon I'd been thinking about how I might get a chance to talk to him. I couldn't afford to pay him so I'd been wondering how to bring up my business problems in a casual conversation. I was desperate; my family, suppliers, clients, and staff were all counting on me. Good old Dave Ettinger, Mr. Superman, needed a hand. What was the point of hiding it anymore?

"Yeah," I said, letting my bulletproof façade fall. "I think I do. My company's in the toilet and I'm almost wishing for it to be flushed once and for all."

Mark chuckled at my analogy.

"In fact, I think I might have that conversation with my wife after the kids go to bed tonight," I said. "Everything's falling apart and I don't know how to turn it around. I think it's over."

"I'll tell you what Dave. Before you throw in the towel let's grab a coffee and talk a bit. Maybe I can help." His eyes turned to the team of twelve year olds in the outfield. "After practice let's meet at the Diamond Café."

"In the meantime, there's no point moping on the bleachers. Besides, the next foul ball may kill you," he laughed.

Then Mark stood up and pointed to a small work site a few hundred feet behind us. "Why don't you go over and give Teru a hand? He's in charge of building the league an indoor batting cage. I'm sure he could use some help."

"Okay," I said, grateful for the chance to get my mind off of business.

"Great," Mark said as he returned to the field. "Tell Teru I sent you over. I could use the brownie points with him!"

7

Teru Yamamoto was a short, heavy set man in his mid sixties. He obviously took care of himself. He was fit, energetic, and always moving. He'd been a volunteer with the West Valley Association for as long as anyone could remember. He was always there but never really noticeable, if you know what I mean. When I coached he stayed in the background, helping out with the fields whenever he was needed. I'm ashamed to say that I never took the time to get to know him. As I walked towards the building site I noticed him next to a pile of lumber. He was hammering nails smoothly and he never seemed to stand still. As I got closer I could see that he was working on the footings for the foundation walls.

"Hey Teru," I said, sticking out my hand. "Mark sent me over. Not sure if you remember me but my name's Dave Ettinger."

"Of course I remember you! Good to see you again, Dave," Teru said, shaking my hand enthusiastically.

"Mark thought I might be able to lend you a hand."

"That would be great! I'm just building the forms for the foundation and I could use some help cutting the lumber. The saw is over there and I've marked all the cuts all ready."

"Sure," I replied, throwing my jacket onto a nearby work bench.

We worked for a few minutes. I was cutting wood and Teru was nailing it into place. Soon I was slipping back into thought, rolling my problems around in my mind over and over again. Why had I told Mark I needed help? What had come over me? What was talking about it going to accomplish? I just wanted the endless sense of dread that the business filled me with to be over.

As if he could hear my thoughts, Teru stopped pounding nails and sat down on the bench next to where I was working.

"So Dave, I can't remember what you do for a living." he said, wiping sweat from his brow with a towel.

"I run a software business," I said.

"Software?" Teru echoed. "That's cool. How's it going for you?"

I swallowed hard. "In all honesty, not great, I'm thinking about shutting the whole thing down. I'm meeting with Mark after practice today to see what he thinks."

Teru looked concerned. "What's wrong with the company?"

"You name the problem, we have it," I said. "No cash flow, high overhead, projects behind schedule and costing more to finish than we charged, our marketing isn't working, upset clients, low staff morale, suppliers are threatening to cut us off, huge debt load. It's a big mess." I went on and on for a good five minutes, sharing the excruciating minutiae of my business issues.

Teru listened patiently then pulled two bottles of water out of a cooler, handed me one, opened the other, and took a swig.

"That reminds me of an old fable. Want to hear it?" he asked.

"Sure," I answered, thinking I had exposed myself too much already. I thought I'd better get in a joke. "Why not? I can't dance and I'm too fat to fly."

"You're a funny guy," Teru said, grinning. He took another drink and then started to talk. "So, a few thousand years ago, back in India, a farmer had three unsuccessful years in a row and was desperate for help. One day he hears about a guru living far up in the mountains who has a reputation for solving problems. The farmer packs up some food and clothes and he sets off to see the guru.

"For eight days and eight nights, the farmer travels through the countryside. As he reaches the base of the mountain, he gets robbed by some highwaymen. It doesn't matter; all he had on him to steal was some food and one extra cloak. The farmer climbs the mountain, finds the guru's cave, and discovers a long lineup of people waiting for help. Some of them shared their extra food and another gave him a spare blanket. The lineup gave the farmer two days to list all of the problems he was going to ask the guru to solve.

"He waits and waits and waits until his turn finally comes. Then he walks into the guru's cave and sits down. The guru was dressed in a simple robe and had a long white beard. He was seated cross-legged on the hard floor of the cave."

"How can I help you?" the guru asks him.

"Well, I've had a long time to think about this," the farmer replies pointing to the lineup behind him, "and I have a list of 82 problems."

"The farmer isn't kidding. He lists out exactly 82 problems: the soil in his field is not as good as his brother's, his wife's a nag, his sons all want to leave the farm to move away, his daughter is sweet on a guy that he thinks is lazy, his cows don't give enough milk, the stream dries up too early every year, a fox

30

keeps killing his chickens, he got mugged on the way here, he's broke, and on and on. After an hour of talking the farmer finally finishes and asks, 'Now, how can you help me with these 82 problems?'"

"Sorry, I can't solve your 82 problems," the guru says calmly.

"The farmer was shocked. 'What?' he says. "It took me eight days just to get here and two more waiting in line. I haven't had a full meal in days and now you say you can't help me with my problems. I don't believe this. What kind of phony guru are you?"

"I can't solve your 82 problems," the guru says, "but maybe I can help you with your 83rd problem."

"Hey wait a minute," the farmer exclaimed. "I thought long and hard to come up with a list of all of all my problems and I only came up with 82. I don't think that I have an 83rd problem!"

"Yes you do," the guru calmly says to him.

Frustrated, the farmer sarcastically asks, "Okay I'll bite. What, EXACTLY, is my 83rd problem?"

"Your 83rd problem is that you don't want any problems. I can help you with that."

Teru leaned back and laughed at his own punch line.

"Dave, I'm pretty sure that if anyone can help you with your business problems, Mark can. But to do it you have to change your attitude towards them. Life will always have problems. Challenges exist in every company, in every relationship, in every endeavor. We have to accept that they are a natural part of the landscape, and we need to remember that life is way too short to get pushed around by your problems. It might be harder to stand up for what you really want, but it's the better route to take."

Teru looked me straight in the eyes to see how I reacted to that statement. I tried to show no fear. I'm not sure that it worked. After a moment he continued.

"Mark has a saying: 'the fastest way to build a strong company is to get good at solving problems.' There are two sides to that statement. If your clients don't have any problems, there's no need for you to build a company to solve them. A surprising amount of companies exist primarily to solve problems for others. It's a good idea to get clear about the problems your company solves. And if building a company was problem-free then there would be too many competitors for you to make a decent profit. In business you have to expect problems and deal with them effectively. It's just part of the package of being a company owner." He paused for a moment, turned his head to survey the forms that we'd been working on, and said, "Mark's got some pretty good ideas when it comes to that stuff."

He took another swig of water and looked at the sun getting lower on the horizon. "We've got to get back to work if we're going to be ready for the rebar tomorrow."

With that Teru stood up and went back to work. I helped as best I could but I was soon lost in thought about what he'd said. He was right. I started thinking about the problems we solve for our clients. I thought that it would be a good idea to make a list of them. It should help improve our marketing and sales presentations.

8

Teru and I worked for another hour before Mark and Ann came over. They inspected our handiwork.

"Wow! Good progress, gentlemen," Mark said.

"It was all Teru," I answered. "The man's a machine."

"Mind if I steal Dave back?" Mark asked Teru.

"No problem," Teru said, winking at me. "I've got it from here. Thanks Dave! I appreciate the help."

"Christine said she'd run Ann home for us," Mark said, pointing to one of the team moms. I recognized her from a couple of years back when her daughter Lisa played on a team I coached. I waved to her.

"Great," I replied. "Ann, be sure to thank Christine and tell Mom that Mark and I are talking business over coffee. I won't be too late."

Mark and I walked to the parking lot and saw the girls off. On the way down Mark asked,

"So what do you think of Teru?"

"You know I've seen him around for years but never took the time to get to know him," I said shaking my head. "I really like him."

"Talk about anything interesting?"

"He told me the story of the 83rd problem."

Mark laughed. "Sounds like Teru. He's got some good stories."

"Yeah," I replied. "And I think he's right. I reached the point where I didn't want any problems anymore. I've been that way for a while now. Every time one comes up it's like hearing fingernails scratching on a chalkboard."

Mark didn't really answer me.

"Teru is pretty incredible," Mark continued. "He's always around keeping the fields in good shape and getting the park ready for games. He's really dedicated to the league. It's his community. He doesn't really say much but he has a great philosophy on life. When he talks, I listen. I mean I really listen, hear what he has to say, and I think it over."

"Yeah, I understand why."

"Let's head over to the Diamond Café," Mark said.

I drove up through the neighborhood, parked in front of the café, and got out. Mark pulled up a minute later and pulled into the spot next to me. As we walked in I remember thinking about how neat the place was. It had been there for about forty years and was one of the jewels of West Valley. It was a throwback to the good old days.

Inside it was set up like a softball diamond. As you walk in home plate is right in front of you, it's the cash register stand with counters coming off at angles, like base paths on a ball diamond. There are five round stools on each of the four sides. The middle of the infield is the servers' area. In the center where the pitcher's circle would be is the milkshake and soda station. The kitchen was at the back and it took up both center field and left field. Right field had eight freestanding tables in it. Up at the front of the restaurant on each side of the door there were three raised booths where the spectator stands would be. From the booths you could look back into the café or out towards the traffic on the street.

As we entered Mark got a warm greeting from the server, Julie. She gave him a big friendly smile before saying, "Hey Mark, it's good to see you again. Where are the kids?" Mark smiled back. I could tell he was happy to see her. "They must have all gone home to do their homework. I just stopped by to have a quick meeting."

"Hi Dave, are you coaching again?" she asked.

I was surprised that she remembered me and even more surprised that she remembered I used to coach. "No, but Ann is playing on Mark's team. I'm surprised you remember me."

"You used to bring your players by and sit on the stools around the infield after some of your games," she replied. "I remember the coaches who are great with their kids and if I remember correctly you always had winning teams by the end of the season. The parents from your teams wouldn't let you pay no matter how hard you tried. Somebody would always beat you here and let me know that they were covering your bill. That kind of stuff is hard to forget."

I smiled at the memories as we settled into a booth along the first base side. Julie brought over a couple of cups of coffee for us and asked, "Is there anything else that I can get you gentlemen tonight?"

"No, I think we're good, unless you want something Mark."

"A cup of your fine coffee is more than enough," he replied with a smile.

"Okay boys, when you need refills give me a holler." She headed off to serve the tables in right field.

Mark looked over at me and started talking. "I want to expand on Teru's story for a bit. Sometimes your problems aren't really problems. It's important to be able to differentiate between problems and symptoms. If difficulties keep coming up regularly then they're most likely the symptoms of underlying problems. Something is probably causing the difficulties to happen. There's likely a cause and effect relationship. For example, if a softball team keeps losing games then I'd start by looking into the coaching and quality of their practices. You'll likely find the real problem there."

"I know what you mean," I said. "I used to play against teams with poor technique and watch the other coaches get frustrated when their players made errors. The real problem was in the practices and if I hear you right the symptoms were in the games."

"That's it," he said. "I'll do the same type of analysis at Velocity. It could be that you have a lot more symptoms than problems and that, strangely enough, would be a good thing. Then we can identify the problems and fix them instead of chasing our tails running after symptoms. They'll go away on their own after the problems are fixed."

9

"So Dave, let's get to your company. You say it's having difficulties, let's call them that for the moment. I'd like to hear more about them." Mark's statement was really more of a question.

"Yup, difficulties, that's putting it mildly," I said as I looked around the café. I didn't really want anybody to know. I was embarrassed by it. There were a few kids seated on the stools around the infield and a couple of full tables over in right field. I didn't look him in the eyes but I'd come this far so I continued on.

"I just can't seem to make it profitable. I bust my hump day after day, week after week, and month after month but the payables just seem to keep growing. I can't even take a decent salary home for myself. Karen and I keep going deeper and deeper into the credit cards and more in debt to the bank just to survive."

"When did you start the company?" he asked.

"About three years ago," I replied.

"Has it always been this way?"

"No, the first year was tough. The second year it looked like we were making some headway, but then last year was brutal. Sales grew but the profits disappeared and I'm working harder than ever.

"Did you change your business model?" Mark asked.

"I'm not sure I know what you mean."

"Okay. One of the first things I try to understand is the business model. If the model is flawed then you won't be able to make it work no matter how hard you try. In that case structural changes are required or maybe it is time to abandon ship. If you've got a sound model and it's not working then it's a performance issue. Sometimes I see a combination of both."

"I'm not following you," I said, wondering why I ever started Velocity Software.

"Well, let me ask you a few more questions. What type of work does your company do?"

"I started out by writing some software that small manufacturers can use. I thought that I could take it to market and the customers would line up. We sold some, but not as many as I expected. It still sells occasionally. Then I started going to networking meetings and taking out ads in the business newspapers letting people know that Velocity could write custom software applications for them and we've gotten some good clients that way. After that our clients asked if we could fix other issues with their computers. Then even more businesses started calling and asking if we could help them so I started a field tech division."

"Tell me a little about the people you've got working a Velocity."

"I've got Patrick, who's been with me since the beginning. He looks after our proprietary software doing the upgrades for the new releases and handles the training. Clients pay us an annual licensing fee, which barely covers his wages. Geoff and Sonya write the custom software. Malcolm, Albert, and Anders are the field techs. The receptionist is Carol and Marcus is the sales rep."

"It sounds like an interesting company and that's a lot of growth in three years. Tell me more about what happened in the beginning."

"I had this idea for the software so I hired Patrick to help me write it. It took longer than I thought so we had to start generating revenues by writing custom software on contract for other people. I brought on Sonya to do that and Geoff followed a bit later. By the end of the year we had a handful of clients for our software and Geoff and Sonya were pretty busy programming for other clients."

"What did you do?" he asked.

"I did some programming, handled the sales, and helped the rest of the programmers with their troubleshooting, that kind of stuff."

"Okay, tell me about year two."

"That's when we started to send field techs out. Our clients were having problems with their computers not related to our software and they asked if we could handle them. I started with a guy named Brad and the money was pretty good so I added another guy. I think Richard was his name. Then things got busy. I was trying to do too many things at once so I hired Marcus as the sales rep. He brought in a bit more work and I hired Anders to be our third field tech. Things were going fairly well at that point. We were bursting at the seams in the original location so I moved Velocity Software to a bigger office and hired Carol to be our receptionist and bookkeeper. I thought the future was starting to look pretty bright, but at the start of year three all hell broke loose."

"Really, tell me about that."

"It started when Brad and Richard decided that they should go out on their own. They slammed Velocity in front of our clients and took some of our best customers with them when they left. They said Velocity was charging them too much and they promised to do the work cheaper."

"Oh crap. What happened next?"

"Brad and Richard screwed some things up and nobody was there to bail them out. They went out of business pretty quick. A few of our old clients came back, mostly because I could get them out of jams. Marcus busted his butt for a while and got some new clients for the field tech business. I hired Geoff and then Albert to do the work and that's where we are now."

"It sounds like you are back where you were a year ago."

"Yeah but there are no profits and I can't figure out why or how to turn it around. The company hasn't started to pay me back for the investment I put in to get the whole thing started. We're not selling much of our own software. It's been a phenomenally tough year and I'm burnt out. I don't think I can work any harder and I'm not sure much will change if I do."

I hung my head looking down at the table. Without looking up I continued. "I'm at the end of my rope. Velocity Software is barely covering its own bills and every month we keep getting further and further behind with the bills at home. The bank lent me some more money today but I'm wondering if I should shut the business down and use it to start my life all over again. I'll probably have to sell the house if I can't get a good paying job quickly and that'll just crush my wife and kids. They love it here."

10

"I think that maybe I can help," Mark said. "I should probably start by explaining what a business model is.

Let's use a softball analogy. Look at the infield in the middle of the Diamond Café. The cash register is where home plate would be. Imagine the customers all coming in at once and paying their money right away. Then the Diamond Café has to supply the meals so they'll need to take money out of the till to pay for the ingredients, the cooks to prepare it, and Julie to serve it. Those are the direct costs; that's what it costs to supply the product and service to the customers. Sometimes direct costs are also called the cost of goods sold, but they're the same thing. The money that's left after those are paid is the gross profit. Gross margin is a different way of describing the same concept. It is gross profit stated as a percentage of revenues.

"Just to be clear, if the revenues are $900 and the direct costs are $600, then gross profit is $300 and the gross margin percentage is calculated by dividing $300 by $900, which is 33%.

"Sometimes people use another system called markup, but I'm not a big fan of that approach. Using this example the markup is 50% because you take the cost, $600, and increase it by 50%, which is $300, to get the revenue of $900.

"The better the gross margin, the better the business model is likely to work. Low margin models need to do a lot more business to generate the same amount of gross profit dollars.

"When the direct costs are covered, the company has reached **first base**. Next they have to take out the money to pay for the overheads like rent, heat, electricity, interest on any debt, credit card fees, marketing and bookkeeping, et cetera. When the overheads are covered then the company has reached **second base**.

"Now Doug, the owner, needs to be paid a fair wage for the work he does. When that happens the company reaches **third base**. If all the money in the till is gone at that point then all Doug has done is create a job for himself and probably not a very good one at that. He's made the investment to get the company started, he's taken all the risk by signing the lease, and if somebody books off sick it's his problem. He's got all the challenges of owning the company, but at third base he's just getting paid like another employee. He may not have a boss, but all he really has is a job working for himself."

"Kind of like softball. If the players only get to third base then the team doesn't score any runs and they can't win the game if they don't score," I said.

"That's right. Scoring is about getting back to **home plate**, or to the till again, with money left over. Profits aren't a dirty word. They can be put back into the company to fuel growth, pay back the initial investment, and provide a reward for the risk that's been taken. Most small companies should be making ten cents of profit, or more, out of every dollar that rolls through the till. That's a reasonable return for the effort that's being put in.

"I'll tell you another thing," he said. "Profitable companies are a lot more fun to own—and a lot better for employees to work at."

He paused to let me take it all in.

"Where do you figure your company is on the bases right now?" Mark asked.

"It depends on the month but I always seem to be getting stuck in the hotbox between second and third. I hardly ever take home a fair wage," I replied.

"That's not too unusual. A fair amount of company owners get caught in that situation at least for a while. I call it the Valley of the Lost Entrepreneurs. A lot of talented people wind up getting lost in there. Some never make it out, but it doesn't have to be that way."

Mark carried on. "The four bases analogy is really a generic description of a business model. To make it your own you need to add in your company promise and consider the scale, which is the amount of business that'll be flowing through the company. The margins and the size of the overheads are also very important components."

I interrupted him. "I haven't heard of a company promise before. What's that?"

"Sorry about that, Dave. I keep forgetting that 'company promise' isn't a very common term, but it really should be. It's the keystone element in any company. It describes the value a company promises to deliver to its prospects and customers.

"Promise?" I asked.

"Sure. A company promise defines the purpose of your company. It's about the value your company is designed to deliver. Successful companies are designed and built to deliver value. A strong company promise has good buy-in from the market and it's also well kept, which means the company delivers on it consistently."

"Buy-in?" I asked a little louder than I should have.

"The market has to want what you are promising and they have to want it enough to pay for it. That's buy-in. Then you're connecting with a viable business opportunity."

"Okay, how do I go about creating a company promise?" I asked.

"A good starting point is to list the products and services you sell and then describe the target market that's willing and able to pay for them. I'll say that again: willing and able to pay. That doesn't mean *wants* to pay. For example, nobody really wants to pay for insurance but almost everybody has at least one type of insurance or another. People are willing to pay for insurance. On the other hand I've seen lots of business models fail because entrepreneurs started out thinking that people would or should pay for their company promise and it turned out that people simply weren't willing to pay. Willing and able to pay is the key. The customers have to buy into your company promise. If they don't, you'll have a real problem on your hands and then you'll experience a boatload of nasty symptoms."

"I can see that."

"Here's where it gets interesting," he said. "Both direct value and collateral value go into the equation. When you build them both into your company promise your chances of success will increase dramatically."

"Can I stop you again for a second?" I asked.

"Sure."

"What do you mean by direct value and collateral value?"

"Well, here at the Diamond for example the direct value is prepared meals brought right to your table. There is good direct value because the food is good. I mean, where else can you get a clubhouse sandwich that uses fresh cooked turkey nowadays? Most other places are using processed meat. Here they cook a turkey almost every day, serve meals with it at dinner time, then make sandwiches and soup with the leftovers the next day. Not to mention the homemade fries here are awesome. Everything on the menu is like that. That's good direct value.

"When it comes to collateral value, they offer friendly service where they remember your name and they're always happy to see you. Their full collateral value package includes even more than that. Look at the walls; they are covered with pictures of kids playing ball. The players love coming in here. The folks here at the Diamond also keep up with the local news. Anybody can come here for a coffee and catch up on what's going on. They really want to connect people into the community. The Diamond has become a hub and they work at keeping it that way. If you need a plumber, don't pick up the Yellow Pages. You're better off to come down here, order a coffee, and let your server know that you need one. The Diamond Café delivers a lot of collateral value.

"Then you need to take your direct value and collateral value and boil it down into a company promise. The Diamond's is great food, community flavor. Everyone who works here knows it and lives by it. They deliver on their company promise all day, every day.

A company promise deliberately chooses the identity of the company. It sets the bar high enough to really take full advantage of the business opportunity."

"I see what you mean," I said. "I've never heard their company promise before but it fits to a T. People come here for more than just the food. They offer good direct value and great collateral value. Both are captured in their company promise." It was starting to all make sense to me.

"I imagined Velocity Software was going to operate something like that when I started it, but I never identified it or wrote it down. We hired lots of people without telling them how I wanted the company to operate or the promise that I wanted them to keep for my clients. No wonder we've been struggling."

"That's true for a lot of companies," Mark replied. "When a company is small with two or three people, how the owner wants the company to operate is clear to everyone involved. But when a company gets larger than that, the connection often gets lost. Having a defined company promise and a plan to consistently reinforce it really helps to keep companies on track. You'll likely have to repeat it over and over until it takes hold with your employees. If it's a good promise though, soon enough it will take on a life of its own."

"I think I can do that and I think I need to do it," I commented.

"You've coached so you'll understand this example," Mark continued. "You can't show up at the first practice of the season and demonstrate the right way to field a ground ball and expect the players to do it properly for the rest of the season. It doesn't work like that—it would be a bit ridiculous to expect good results."

I laughed out loud at how obvious that was.

"Dave, having a well understood company promise that your target market buys into is at the core of a good business model. When you have a strong one that connects well with a good market and you consistently keep it, the sky's the limit. Then it's easy to grow the business and build your company. That's why I call it the keystone element."

"Got it, thanks Mark!"

"What I've also noticed is that when companies don't have company promises they don't consistently deliver the full value they're capable of. It's almost like they stop short for some unknown reason and everything settles to the lowest point of equilibrium. I see a lot of companies that could easily do better, but don't. Having a strong company promise that's a bit challenging to keep will bring good energy into your company, especially when you're excited about it."

"I'd love to have that, but I'm wondering if my employees will buy into it," I said.

"Anytime you raise the bar and set a new standard, you're likely to get some pushback. But think of the alternative. Not having a company promise sentences your company to a lifetime of delivering second class value. Your clients don't want that, even though some may live with it, and I'm sure that's not what you personally want for your company."

"You're right. That's not what I want now and it's definitely not what I wanted when I started Velocity."

"Dave, try looking at it from this perspective. There's a difference between a team and a group. A group is a few or more people doing related activities. A team is defined by winning together and losing together. If you want your company to be a team, the first thing you have to do is tell them what the win is."

"The win is consistently keeping the company promise," I said.

"That's right. There's also another secret ingredient. Are you ready for this?" Mark asked.

"Sure," I replied, wondering what was coming next.

"It's curiosity. They're really good with it here. They've figured out how to use it and everybody is expected to participate."

"Really, how does that work?" I asked.

"Knowing when to use curiosity is important. If somebody comes here and just wants to sit in a booth, order some food, and read the paper or watch the traffic go by, that's okay. If that's not the case then it's the server's role to figure out how the customer interacts with the community and a little bit about what's going on in their life, in a friendly manner of course.

"Another way Doug uses it is to have everybody here on the lookout for what people really enjoy eating. He wants to know if there is any way to make the menu better.

"The other application is that they're curious about ways to improve their customers' experience. Doug was telling me that last year Julie suggested they have a batch of chocolate chip cookie dough in the fridge ready to be baked. Now when parents are having difficulties getting their kids to eat, she can offer to put a cookie into the oven for them—if they eat their food up."

"That's a really neat idea."

"Active use of curiosity is the foundation of a lot of things." He paused. "I know I'm giving you a lot to think about in a short period of time, but stay with me a bit longer."

There was no chance of me drifting off. I was starting to understand things clearly for the first time in since I started Velocity Software.

"Here's something to be curious about: the customers have to appreciate the value that the company offers and the company has to appreciate the value it delivers. When I say that the customers have to appreciate the value, I mean that they have to be willing to part with their money for it. When I say the company has to appreciate their value, I mean that they have to always be looking for ways to increase their value package and to consistently deliver on their company promise. A healthy curiosity about the value your company delivers will serve you well.

"Doug really works the curiosity angle and it goes beyond the value that the company is set up to deliver. One of the big things to be curious about with a business model is the numbers. The first base numbers are very important. How many customers do you need to average per day to turn a net profit? How often do they need to come back and buy again? What's the average sale from each visit going to be? What gross margin do you need? How will that in turn impact your revenues? You have to know those numbers to analyze the business model.

"Plus, I always like to know if the products and services are easy to sell. That makes a real difference in how difficult it is to make a business model work. If there are people already looking to buy then there's already an established demand in the marketplace and you're dealing with active buyers. In that case you're likely to be competing with other companies for the business. To keep your margins up, you'll likely have to offer good collateral value and work in the top end of the market.

"You have passive buyers when you have to get out there and create the demand. That means you have to educate the market as to why they are better off with your products and services before they'll buy. In that case the marketing plan is more intricate, but the margins will probably be higher.

"Pricing also plays a key role here. One way to increase the value delivered is to drop the prices so your customers can get the same products and services for less money, hence better value. More often than not though, this is not a very practical approach. If you're going to use this strategy you'll need to have lower costs yourself, either by reducing direct costs or overheads, or you'll need more volume from increased customer visits or a larger average dollar sale per visit. Dropping prices generally means you're going to have to work harder to make the same amount of gross profit. It's tough to build a business model in the low end of the market that's capable of winning over the long haul."

Mark paused to let that sink in.

"Given all that, what changed at Velocity Software?" he asked.

"Well, we took on some more work, moved to a bigger office space, hired a receptionist, and brought on a sales rep," I said.

"I'll bet you don't bill out as many of your own hours anymore."

"You're right there. I used to bill out twenty hours a week but now I'm so busy putting out the fires my employees cause I don't think I've even billed out an average of five lately."

"Did anything happen with your pricing and your margins?" he asked.

"We did drop our prices, but not intentionally. To get the old clients back we had to give them a bit of a deal and when Marcus was trying to build the field tech business back up again he came to me regularly asking for discount pricing so he could land new clients," I replied.

"What about the direct costs? Are you as efficient at delivering the services as you used to be?"

"I don't know for sure but I don't think so. I know we're running over on some of the custom software contracts and I can't believe the number of problems that are coming in from the field techs. We can't charge the clients when the field techs are waiting on-site for me to call them back to help diagnose and solve the problems. Traffic on the roads is also getting worse so there's more time wasted on travel. Some of our clients are pretty far away from the office now."

"Yeah, that's what I figured," Mark said. "Before you were getting more runners onto first base and your margins were better. Margins are important to business models. Your overheads used to be lower and that made it easier to get to second base. Because you used to personally put more time into billable work, you were covering part of your own wages, which made third base easier too. It sounds like some months you might have even scored a few runs."

"Yeah, I wish that I could get back there. Even if I could I'd still want to make some improvements. It wasn't heaven but it sure wasn't the hell I'm going through now!"

"I think we can get you close in the next ninety days," Mark said thoughtfully. "The next step is to do a forecast and variance report. It will identify the symptoms, and it will help us locate the problems and fix them."

"What's a forecast and variance report," I asked.

"It should be a central part of your financial information systems. It's basically numerical representation of your business model. It shows you how money flows through your company which is kind of important. I'd like to get working on it right away. Are you available in the morning?"

"Yeah, I'll make time for this if it'll help. I'll have Carol, our receptionist, sit in as well. She does the bookkeeping."

"That's good. How's her time? Is she really busy or can we give her some work to do over the next couple of days?"

"I suspect that she spends a fair amount of her time doing stuff just to look busy. I mean, she's a good employee and all, but I don't really give her enough direction."

"How does 8:00 AM sound to you?"

I hesitated. "It sounds good, but first I need to know how much this is going to cost me," I said, wondering if my new bank loan would cover it.

"I'm not thinking about money right now. I'd like some of your time. Teru needs a hand with the batting cage construction and in the long run I'd like to see you coaching ball again. That doesn't mean that I won't ever be invoicing you, but for now we can just trade time."

"That sounds really good to me. Do you think it's going to work out?" I asked hopefully.

"Call it a coach's hunch," Mark said. "Every year at the first practice I ask the kids to name the best coach they ever had. This year, half of my team said you, Dave."

"Yeah, I coached for three of four years and quite a few of your players were on my team at one time or another. That seems like a long time ago, back when I had time for things like coaching."

"I've never had so many kids give me the same answer, so I figure you must be all right," Mark chuckled. "Usually, I get twelve different answers from twelve different kids.

"I like to ask them that question to get a discussion going about what makes a good coach. Once that's clear, I find they're more involved when we start talking about what makes a good team player. Next I lead a discussion about what the league's slogan 'Everybody Wins' means. It sets the stage for the type of season we want to have." He stopped and rubbed his chin.

"I think we'll find some ways to tweak your business model and get you back on track. If you bring the same skill set that the kids seem to approve of and work with the practice plans I set out for you, everything should work out just fine."

PART THREE

As Told By Jen

11

Mr. Ettinger stood up in his office and said, "Wow Jen, we've been at this for a while."

I looked at my watch. It was 5:30. Where had the time gone? I was fascinated by his story and there were so many questions floating in my mind. "Dave, do you have to leave now?" I asked.

"Not right away Jen. I can stay a bit longer, but I need to stretch my legs and I wouldn't mind getting a glass of water. How about you, would you like one too?"

"Water would be excellent. I should hit the road by six, if that's okay."

"Sure, let's walk down to the coffee room."

On the way down Dave started talking again. "Over the next few months I often found myself wishing that I'd met Mark a year earlier, before I got the company into such a mess. But now looking back on it, I wouldn't trade the experience for anything. The lessons I learned really stuck and Velocity Software has always been stronger for it." Dave's face broke out into a big grin and he shook his head. "I wouldn't wish it on anybody else though. Life is funny that way."

As we approached the coffee room he said, "Why don't we just stay in here, that way we can put our feet up and relax."

He opened the cupboard, got two glasses out, and continued reminiscing.

"Mark was a pretty sharp guy. He didn't want to overload me with information. At first he was using the AR²T of momentum without telling me about it. He was working his way through the assessment phase and getting an idea about the results I wanted. He was already realizing the options we had to move forward and he had a TRaction plan ready to go for the morning. It was amazing how fast he pieced it together.

"Here's your water," he said as he handed me a glass and took a sip from his own. He settled into a chair, and swung his feet up onto another. It struck me again how much he made me feel just as important as he was. We were just two people hanging out, having a conversation.

51

"Jen, so far we've covered two of the five key elements: the AR²T of momentum, and the Company Promise. When we get back to Velocity's story it's going to dive right into the third element, Financial Information Systems. They're about managing and growing a company's profitability."

Dave swung his feet down off of the chair and turned towards me.

"Jen, choices are harder to make because you don't always know the 'how' when you make them. In general people don't like that kind of uncertainty. Sometimes to get certainty people trade off what they really want and decide to settle for less. The idea is to make good choices and keep the AR²T forms open with consistent TRaction until you get the results you want. It really helps to have somebody like Mark around giving you ideas and keeping the AR²T forms up on your radar. I probably wouldn't have been able to design and build a company like this without him."

"Whatever happened to Mark?" I asked.

"He's still with us but age is starting to take his mind and his health is failing. I visit him as often as I can. Sometimes he seems to be all there, other times not so much. He has a lot better memory for the old days than for things that happened yesterday. He's in a home now since his wife passed away. It's the West Valley Gardens and we got him into a unit that looks over the ballpark."

"That's sad. I mean it's nice that he can see the ball games and all but it's too bad about his wife passing and his health failing."

Both of us took a drink of water and I changed the subject.

"Dave, why do you think it's so difficult to find information for this project?"

He smiled and shook his head. "How to be successful in business is not as well understood as it should be, especially when you consider our economy depends on it.

"Before I met Mark I didn't know what I didn't know. Over the years I've seen a lot of good people go into business only to find themselves in the same situation I'd gotten myself into. It's too bad there aren't more Marks to go around, but perhaps by telling you the story you'll find a way to include his five key elements in your whitepaper. I know they'll help a lot of people and it's important to me that they get written down and shared."

"From what I've heard so far I think they'll definitely help a lot of company owners. Can I ask a question coming from a different angle though?"

"Sure, fire away."

"What are some common mistakes that company owners make?"

"Well, in a wide open market growth is almost irresistible. The Supersize Syndrome sets in. People think more is better and owners chase revenue growth without really thinking it through. Growth and dreams of growth almost become an obsession. The 'bigger is better' mindset is pretty seductive."

"Isn't growth good in business?" Up until now everything he said made sense, but now I was hearing that growth isn't a part of the equation. This didn't seem to make sense to me. Growth has to be good."

"If you've got growth that can be a good sign, but other times you see that sign on a dead end road," he explained. "I've learned to be cautious when people are excited to tell me how much their business is growing. Growth can expose a lot of problems. The secret is to know what's causing the growth. If it's because the company is getting stronger and better at delivering on its company promise, then it's a good thing. If it's because the market opportunity is getting bigger or they're just spending more money on marketing to get in front of extra customers, then there is certainly some risk involved. Particularly if they are getting their new business because of lower prices and they don't have a structural cost advantage over their competitors. You need to understand the reason for the growth and make sure it's sustainable. Can I take a minute here?"

"Take as long as you need," I replied. I started making myself look busy by flipping through my pages and pages of notes. After a bit I looked up. He leaned in and started talking again.

"It's more important to keep an eye on your profits. When people chase revenue growth, the profits don't always follow naturally. In fact, they can go in the opposite direction. When the companies haven't been strengthened enough to handle the increased business, their capabilities easily get swamped and they become inefficient. The end result is often more work for less profit—that's a lot more common than you think."

"Profits should fuel the growth, not the other way around. If companies need to grow their business to become profitable then they're vulnerable. Mark's advice was always to get profitable now, learn how to stay profitable, and then grow from there."

Dave continued. "Anytime you see a company that's constantly fighting fires and has cash flow difficulties then it's pretty safe to assume that the company is not strong enough to handle the business it's trying to process."

"That makes sense," I said.

"If the problem is a weak company promise, a poor marketing plan, or a combination of both then you might find the company doing business with anyone who has a credit card. Mark calls that 'Chasing the Dragon' which, believe it or not, is a term that originally came from heroin addicts. They use it as a metaphor for shooting up their drugs. Companies that are chasing the dragon are taking business that doesn't match their strengths or they're dropping their prices too low to get the business. It might feel good at the time and bring some cash in to pay the bills, but it's not a healthy long-term strategy."

"No kidding," I said.

"Mark always brought an interesting perspective to things."

"How do you think that he got so good at coaching company owners?" I asked.

"I've been asking Mark that myself lately and I am not getting the answers I'm looking for. When someone is good at what they do it's often difficult for them to describe how they actually do it."

Dave laughed and then added something that suddenly made a lot of things clear. "I think that you've got a fascinating project here. If it doesn't tax your brain then the findings won't be of much value. It's not like you're going to turn over a rock and find your answer. I just don't think it's going to work like that. Finding simplicity on the other side of complexity is more about the journey than the destination. You have to do the work and earn it.

"The people reading your whitepaper will also need to work with the concepts before they find their own simplicity on the other side of complexity. I think your job is to give them a roadmap and show them what needs to be worked on. Most owners want to build strong companies. They just aren't clear on how to go about it."

"I think you're right," I said.

"Well, it's almost 6:00 and you have to go. Why don't we meet again on Thursday at 2:30 this time? Then we can get into the next part of the story. I think you'll find it to be pretty interesting."

I agreed and went over to the sink to put our glasses in.

We walked back down the hall to his office where I collected the rest of my things. We chatted casually as we made our way to our vehicles in the parking lot.

12

I arrived early the next morning at Carey Jones Norton. Alice was already there and Mr. Jones was in his office with the door closed as usual. A couple of the accountants were also at their desks already working hard.

"I'll make the coffee this morning," I said cheerfully to Alice. "How are you doing today?"

"I'm a bit tired," she responded. "I've been taking evening courses and last night I was up until 2:00 AM studying for an exam coming up on Friday."

"Really, what are you studying?" I asked as we walked down towards the coffee room.

"Accounting. I've been working at it for a couple of years. I'd like to move up in the company someday. Wow, I sure could use my coffee this morning."

"Me too, I was up late last night as well. I feel like I'm finally making some headway on this project of mine. Hey, has anybody around here noticed that you're taking courses."

"No, they don't pay that much attention to me. I mean they're polite and all, but this is a head down and butt up kind of company. It's all about getting your work done and moving on to the next billable job."

We continued to make small talk as I made a pot of coffee.

"You know, I'm not sure I should tell you this, but people around here are starting to talk about you," she said. "It seems like you're not under the gun to produce billable hours like they are, and lately you haven't been around much to help them out. If I was you I'd forget about your project for a while and chip in a bit more. They don't get what you're doing and some of them see it as a bit of a wild goose chase."

Her comments stopped me in my tracks. I'd noticed that people were more cordial and less friendly recently but I'd been too caught up in my own project to give it much thought.

"Thanks for the heads up," I said. I was thinking that the concepts I'd gotten from Dave will really impress Mr. Jones. Now I needed to roll them out to my test clients and see how well they are received and if they get implemented. I made a mental note to request a meeting with Mr. Jones on Friday afternoon. Today was Wednesday and I was meeting with Dave again on Thursday afternoon. That gave me today and tomorrow morning to meet with my company owners and it left Friday morning open to prepare a report.

Suddenly I became anxious. I wanted to get to my desk right away and prepare a good agenda for the meetings with my five clients. There was a lot to cover and I had to boil it down and sound professional when I met with them.

"I've got to get going, I hope you don't mind. I'm just going to take a cup out of the middle," I said as I pulled the pot out from the machine and slid my mug under the stream of coffee that was still coming down.

It only took a few seconds. I slid the pot back into the machine and I was on my way. "Have a great day," I said, trying to sound cheerful. It didn't work very well.

"Jen, I'm sorry. I didn't mean to upset you. I was just trying to help."

"That's okay. I didn't take it the wrong way and I appreciate you mentioning it."

I got to my desk as quickly as I could. The computer seemed to take forever to fire up. *Come on, come on*, I was thinking. The first thing I did was e-mail Mr. Jones to ask him for a meeting on Friday at 3:00 PM.

Then I e-mailed the five companies and set appointments with them as well, two for this afternoon and three for tomorrow.

Next I opened a Word document and wrote 'Agenda' on the top of the page. I clicked down a few lines to put in the first topic. Ideas started to swirl around in my mind and they wouldn't stop. AR^2T of momentum, company promise, direct value, collateral value, pricing, choose, decide, learning zone, a company does business in a market, 83rd problem, supersize syndrome, chasing the dragon, financial information systems, business model, first base, second base, third base, home. Why wouldn't my brain stop spinning around? Where should I start? I didn't know. I couldn't think straight.

Oh man, what did I just do to myself?

After half an hour of mostly just staring at the screen, I picked up the phone.

"Is Mr. Ettinger there, please?"

"No, he's out of the office today in meetings. Would you like his voicemail?"

My heart sank. I drifted off in silence.

"Is there anybody else that can help you?" the receptionist, Iola, asked in a friendly voice.

Maybe Stan will give me Dave's number. "Is Stan in?"

"I'll try his line for you. Thanks for calling Velocity Software."

After three rings I heard, "Stan here. How can I help you?"

His voice was a ray of hope. "Stan, it's Jen. Do you have Dave's number? I need to talk to him," I blurted out.

"Hi Jen, I do but don't expect he'll answer it today. It sounds a bit urgent. Is there anything that I can help you with?"

"I don't think so." I dropped my head into my hands. I felt like crawling under my desk. I was on top of the world on the way in to work and now I just wanted to disappear into thin air.

"Why don't you give me a try anyways?" Stan asked. "Occasionally I can make myself useful."

Before I knew it I started talking and the whole story just poured out. As I was finishing I looked over at the clock on the wall. Nine o'clock! How could I have gotten things so far sideways so fast?

"Hmm, take a few deep breaths and calm down a bit."

There was silence on the line. "Stan, are you still there?" He was my only lifeline at this point and I didn't want to lose him.

"Yeah, I'm here. I'm just thinking it through." He paused again. "Tell me what you know about the AR²T of momentum."

I flipped through my notes and found the page as fast as I could. "Basically the A stands for **Assessment**, the first R is for **Realize the Results you want**, the second R is for **Realize the Available Options** and the T is for **TRaction,** which is towards results action."

"Okay, that's a good place to start. I'm e-mailing you a form as we speak. Can you check for it?"

I opened my browser. A few e-mails came in while I was on the phone. All together there were three of them, one from Mr. Jones and two responses from clients. I couldn't help myself. I clicked open the reply from Mr. Jones. It was short, but it didn't look too sweet to me: Friday is good, make it 3:30 instead of 3:00 PM.

Ba dunk, the e-mail from Stan arrived. "I've got it! I'm just opening it now."

All it had was an attachment and I opened it right away. It was a one page AR²T form. "I've got it here in front of me."

"Let's take the shortcut through this, starting with the A. You're in the panic zone and you've got five appointments to present material that you really aren't comfortable with. You have to prepare a report on the meetings by Friday afternoon and that doesn't leave much time for the clients to implement anything. Can you write that down in the top box for me?"

"I can but I'm not sure that I want to," I said as I shook my head.

"Jen, hang in there with me. If you're going to have any chance of getting through this you've got to work through the steps. Even if the picture is ugly, the best path is always to know where you're at, the results you want to get, and the options that you have available. Then you can choose the best course of TRaction."

"I'll give it my best shot. I'm not sure it's going to do any good though."

Ignoring my comment, he continued. "Now let's move to the first R. I should tell you that sometimes it's necessary to re-evaluate here. Let's start with the target of making the Friday meeting. If it doesn't look doable based on the available options perhaps you should consider rescheduling. For now, let's run with it and see if we can make it work. Write down: 'have five good meetings and impress Mr. Jones with a report on Friday.'"

"Do you think that's realistic?"

"Maybe, let's look at the options. What do you think they are?"

"I don't know!" I said, perhaps with a bit too much frustration in my voice. "Sorry Stan, I know you're trying to help here, but I just don't know."

"Okay, in the realize the results box it starts with 'have five good meetings.' If you start solving a problem for somebody, they'll likely think that it's a good meeting. I don't think that we need to set the bar too high by aiming at resolving all their issues right then and there."

"Okay, I'm with you. I appreciate you helping me with this."

"Well, I've never met them and I don't even know who they are, so I'm not sure how much more I can pitch in. I'll have to think about it," Stan said.

I closed my eyes, took a deep breath, and thought, *I'm still stuck in this mess by myself.*

"What I would do, if I was you, is start by printing out more copies of the AR^{2}T form that you're writing on and think about each of the companies. Write their biggest business problem in the assessment box. If you don't know it, phone and ask them. Actually, it's probably a good idea to identify their top three problems. That way you won't box yourself in too much. It will give you more opportunities to find something that they can implement and make progress with."

It seemed to be a good way to start but I wasn't comfortable yet so I waited for him to continue.

"Okay, get working on that and if you need more help, call me back," he said.

A wave of relief flowed over me. "Stan, you're a saint. I don't know how to thank you."

He laughed. "Well, I think you owe me at least a coffee here. Before I let you go and get to work I should caution you that when you're filling out the AR²T forms for your clients the assessment and realize the results boxes are the most straightforward to fill out. The realize the available options and TRaction boxes can be more challenging."

"I'm sensing that right now," I said.

"Did Dave tell you the two magic questions if you get stuck on the second R?"

I started flipping through my notes again. "I've got them! "If you don't know the answers, who do you know that might,' and 'if you did know how to get the results, what would you know?'"

"Alright, you're good to go for a while. I'll be in all day; don't be afraid to call."

"I'll be talking to you soon." I looked at the clock again. 9:30 AM? This was some kind of day!

13

My first appointment was at 11:00 AM with Ben from ABC Landscaping. I arrived with three AR²T forms and spent the first ten minutes discussing the AR²T of momentum with him. For the next hour or so we filled them out as best we could. It seemed to work more easily when we started by filling out the first R, realize the results you want. I used my journalism skills to ask good questions and draw his choices out.

Even then it was apparent that he really hadn't thought about the choices he wanted to make all that clearly before. He said he wanted to get ABC Landscaping to the next level and I had to probe a bit to discover what that actually meant. I kept asking questions until his thoughts crystallized.

Then we turned to the first AR²T form. He chose reducing his time on the tools to twenty hours per week as the results he wanted. The remainder of his time would be shared between being in the office, inspecting the quality of the work his two crews were doing, and making sales calls to find enough new clients to add a third crew.

Ben also described how several of his competitors had grown from the level he was at, with dreams of building huge businesses, only to downsize back to a couple of crews again. He believed it was because of the difficulties they had maintaining quality workmanship as they grew. It sounded to me like they should have developed strong company promises and kept them.

The second AR²T form concentrated on getting some commercial clients who would provide ABC with stable year-round work.

On the third AR²T form we listed hiring another good crew and having them consistently perform to ABC's standards.

We went back through the forms, this time looking at the assessment and realize the options boxes. On the first AR²T form the assessment was that at the current time he needed to be on the job billing out most of his time during the day while doing the office work in the evening. Sales calls were fit in around the work and most of his crew oversight was done over the phone, which Ben wasn't comfortable with. He's pretty sure that their work was alright but at the same time he didn't believe it was up to his high standards. We put developing a company promise and entertaining the two magic questions into the realize the options box. Ben agreed to think about them some more and also discuss them with his staff. It all went into the TRaction plan.

We discussed the other AR²T forms briefly, but pretty soon he had to get back to business or his day's work wouldn't get done. We agreed to meet again next week.

At two in the afternoon I met with Ron from Waltham Signs. I started by describing the AR²T of momentum again. Ron was a bit more skeptical. I even tried using different words. If you knew where you were, knew where you wanted to be, had some creative ideas to close the gap and then got TRaction, you should get where you want to go.

He kept saying that he got the concept but wasn't sure that it would work in his situation. He'd tried everything he could think of but somehow the business didn't ever get much past breakeven. He felt that's just the way it was in the sign industry.

I didn't know where to take the conversation so I ended the meeting early and headed to my car. I sat in the parking lot for a few minutes before calling Stan.

"Jen, how are you doing?" He asked as soon as he picked up the phone, "I've been waiting for your call."

"Well, I've been better," I responded quietly. "I get the AR²T of momentum in my mind but it's hard to make it work in the real world."

He laughed. "You don't have much experience with it yet so I wouldn't expect miracles. Why don't you tell me about your appointments today?"

"It started off not too bad. Ben from ABC Landscaping had some patience with me and we started filling out the AR²T forms, although they were a bit light on second R, the realize your options part. Then we were even thinner on the TRaction plans."

I paused for a bit and Stan didn't say anything. "Ben is going to start thinking about a company promise. We also discussed how he could get some more time in the office to manage his company. I suggested that he think about who he knew who might know the answer and also to consider if he did know how to get that result, what he would know. We're both going to talk to some other people and meet again next week. I've got some hope there. If he wasn't so busy we could have made more progress."

"That sounds like a good start," he said, trying to sound cheerful.

"Stan, can I ask you a question?"

"Sure, go ahead."

"Ben asked me if the company promise was like a Mission Statement. I told him that a company promise is more about the personality of a company and the value it delivers. I agreed to check into it, but I think a mission statement is more about where the company is going. Is that right?"

"That's actually pretty close. There's another piece of the puzzle. At Velocity Software our Vision Statement is about where the company is going, our mission statement is how we plan to get there and our company promise is who we have to be in order to get there. I think the company promise is by far and away the most important one of the three. The vision and mission statements are just words on a page if you don't keep your promise."

"Okay good. After that I went to see Ron from Waltham Signs. He was a real hard case. He said that he could understand the process, but didn't think that it would work in his business. He kept complaining about how bad the customers were, always grinding him on price and taking their business somewhere else to save a buck." I sighed. "We didn't get anything down for options and absolutely nothing into the TRaction plan."

"Sometimes that happens," Stan said. "People can only work a problem for so long without getting any results before they just start to give up and assume that there aren't any solutions. Progress and motivation always seem to go together."

"Tomorrow I'm seeing Martin from Hydro Plumbing at eight in the morning, followed by Grant from West Valley Auto Repair at ten, then Ray from the St. John Pub at 12:30 before I meet with Dave at 2:30. Boy, will he be surprised at how big of a pickle that I've got myself into." I chuckled a bit without really feeling it.

"I've been able to clear some time on my schedule tomorrow morning. Would you mind if I tagged along to your first two appointments?" Stan asked.

"That would be awesome." For a moment I couldn't believe that he would volunteer but I was starting to understand that the people around Velocity Software operated on a different wavelength.

"I sure appreciate you taking the time. It'll be a real relief to have somebody along."

"No problem. Dave's back in tomorrow and I'm pretty sure that he can handle anything that comes up around here," Stan said. "I'll call him tonight and I'll give him an overview of where you're at, to kind of soften the blow for your 2:30 meeting. Is there anything else in your notes that might help us out in the meetings tomorrow?"

"I was thinking about that and it might be interesting to ask some questions about their business models. It also blends right into the four bases concept. I probably should have asked Ben and Ron where they were on the bases right now. Maybe we can also ask some better questions around their company promises and discuss them in more depth. Most owners aren't familiar with the concept. Dave says it's the keystone element and I'd like to make sure the clients understand it."

"That's a good idea. Let's stay with Ben and Ron for a bit here. You've talked about them both for a while now. What do you think about their business models?"

"Ben and ABC Landscaping take care of properties so people have time to do other things. I imagine some of his clients don't have the skill or inclination to do it for themselves. I think he's getting around third on the bases mostly because he's doing a lot of work himself. It looks like he needs more volume or higher margins to reach his goal of being more of a company manager."

"Are you sure that he's really getting around third? It sounds to me like he's putting in a lot of time as an unpaid manager. He's doing most of managerial work after hours and he's probably not charging the company for those hours. If he paid himself fairly, for all the time he puts in, I doubt he'd be getting to third."

"You know, you might be right. I'll have to ask some questions around that when we get together next week," I replied.

"Ron on the other hand is a bit different. They make signs and it appears that all of the value is in the products. People order from him because they don't have the equipment to make the signs themselves and Ron is stuck with a lot of competitors in his market."

"That business can be tough, but he needs to find a way to build some more value around his products and come up with a good company promise," Stan commented.

"Yeah, you're right! That's the collateral value that Dave was talking about. If he could tap into something there it would help him to separate himself from his competition. That would get him away from competing on price all of the time. It's driving him nuts."

"A 'me too' type of business is a real challenge to make profits with and if that's what he sees Waltham Signs as then it's no wonder he's getting frustrated."

"How can we get him past that?" I wondered aloud.

"It might be a good idea to interview some of his clients. Perhaps you can get some clues there."

"Okay, that sounds like a good idea. At least it puts something in the TRaction plan for his company. I'll call and ask him to get a few names ready."

"Great. I know where Hydro Plumbing's shop is so I'll meet you there at a quarter to eight tomorrow. That'll give us a few minutes to prepare before we go in."

"Thanks Stan, have a good night," I said as I was thinking about finding some time to review my notes from my meetings with Dave. I thought that it might not be a bad idea to go through the box of materials I got from Mr. Jones as well. I figured that I really needed to get some wins in my meetings tomorrow.

14

The next morning I arrived at Hydro Plumbing at 7:40 AM. That gave me a few minutes to collect my thoughts from the evening before. I wanted to focus on the business model a bit more by presenting the baseball analogy and drilling into how clearly Martin saw the value his company delivers. It would be good if we could help him arrive at a company promise.

From my previous conversations with him I knew he was pretty frustrated with his crews. They always seemed to take more time to complete the jobs than he allowed for in his quotes. Most of Hydro's work was in new construction and they always appeared to have lots of work on the go, perhaps too much because Martin spent a lot of time on the phone talking to contractors about when he could get back to their construction sites to finish the work.

I'd printed out the AR²T forms and wrote sub-par crew performance in the assessment box on the first one, but I figured that might be a bit harsh to write down before I discussed it with him so I crumpled it up and got out a fresh sheet. I didn't use Stan's idea of calling my clients to find out what their top three problems were. I was hoping he wouldn't say anything.

At exactly 8:45 Stan rolled into the parking lot in his black Chrysler 300. Once again he was a sight for sore eyes.

He got out and walked over to my Honda Civic and jumped into the passenger seat.

"How are you on this fine morning?" he asked with a smile.

"I'm good," I replied. I brought him up to speed with my thinking.

"That sounds great," he said. "It's in line with the questions Dave was asking when I talked to him last night. He'd like to see the AR²T forms when you meet with him this afternoon. He also wanted me to make sure that we asked questions to understand their business models and to find out where their companies are on the bases. He also talked about company promises and getting a sense of the direct and collateral value they offer. He even mused about whether or not their choices are getting lost in their decisions."

Stan paused. "I would have thought that Martin would be pretty busy at this time in the morning," he said.

"The crews get here at about 7:00 AM," I replied. "He wants them on the sites and working by 8:00, but a couple of them just left a few minutes ago. I know that they stop at the suppliers on their way to the work sites most mornings. It drives him crazy how much time they waste."

At 7:55 we headed in. I introduced Stan to Peter, Hydro's Service Manager, who invited us to pour ourselves a coffee while Martin dealt with a few problems that were coming in via his phone.

When he finally got to us at 8:20 he started by apologizing. "I don't know why I ever book appointments at this time. The crews should be out on the sites and working by now but they seem to start almost every day by finding more problems than they solve."

He turned to his Service Manager and said, "Hold all of my calls except for Clay and Marshall. I need to know how their jobs are going."

It was a good meeting, except for the frequent interruptions. It seemed like nobody in the company could move without talking to Martin and he was constantly complaining that they couldn't figure things out for themselves.

We started discussing the value that Hydro Plumbing delivered and Martin figured that it was all about the direct value of doing the job for the lowest price, meeting the construction schedule, and handling the inspection deficiencies quickly. Martin was having difficulty absorbing the concept of collateral value. Stan said that was why Martin thought he had to compete on price.

Martin made some notes when we talked about developing a company promise. Lowest price, there when you need us, and done right were his big three. He commented that if he already had a company promise that's what it would be. Then he shook his head and remarked that it was a tough one to keep. Stan said that it reminded him of an old saying. 'You can have the lowest price, the best service, or the highest quality: pick any two.' Martin smiled and agreed to do some more thinking about it.

When we told him about the softball metaphor and asked him where he thought he was on the bases, Martin was pretty certain that a plumber with his ability and experience could make a lot more money than he was currently making working for himself. In fact, a few of his guys were regularly taking home more than he was. At the same time he said that he couldn't imagine working for anybody else ever again. He liked being in control of his time. That seemed a bit strange to me because I knew that he was working over sixty hours a week and a few weeks earlier his wife, Sandra told me that Hydro had almost completely taken over his life.

Then we got three AR²T forms going. On the first one we put getting all the crews to be more accountable and responsible like Craig his lead man was. He wanted all his people to do more thinking about the whole job and then to hustle and get the work finished so they wouldn't have to make extra trips back to the job sites. That really played havoc with the schedule board. Way too many jobs were running long and he often wound up going to job sites himself to complete the work and keep the company on schedule.

The assessment here was that a couple of his crews just didn't seem to care enough. They said they did but their actions told Martin another story.

When we started filling out the realize the options box on the AR²T form some good ideas came forward. The first was keeping the schedule board on the office wall up to date. That way the crews could get a better understanding of the upcoming work and they'd know why it was important to finish their jobs on time. Second was having them go over the layouts and developing their plan of attack for their jobs every morning before they left for the sites. If all the crews were there together they could learn from each other. This would also allow Martin to make some suggestions before the work got behind. Third was developing a workable company promise and making sure it was kept. Another was keeping the truck inventories stocked up to reduce the amount of trips to the suppliers. Every night when the crews came back someone would be assigned to take a look at the stock levels in all the vans. They would check to see what needed to be replenished. A combined order could be e-mailed to the supplier at the end of the day. Then one person could pick up it all up on their way to Hydro's shop for 7:00 AM.

Everything went straight into the TRaction plan, which essentially meant that it would be done within a week.

The second AR²T form was focused on making more profits. Martin really liked the idea of paying himself a fair wage and having the company keep ten cents out of every dollar in profit. I wrote his choice down in the realize the results box.

In the assessment box we wrote 'barely breaking even with the payables rising almost every month'. Again I'm not sure that I quite understood that but it's what Martin wanted written down.

Moving down to the realize the options box we put down 'collect the receivables faster, add a twenty four hour emergency line for high margin calls, get more renovation work directly from homeowners for the same reason, fire some of Hydro's overly demanding contractor clients, and improve the crews' efficiency'. At Stan's urging, developing a company promise was included once again as well as defining Hydro's collateral value. Other options were to improve his quoting process to ensure everything needed for the jobs was detailed and included in the price. We also discussed adding the extra step of job costing after the work was completed to double check and make sure the quoting process was accurate.

On the TRaction plan here we put down 'meet with the guys to figure out a pager schedule, hire an answering service to take the after-hours calls, place ads in the local newspapers, change the Web site, and buy Internet Ad words to target the repair and renovation work'.

The rest of the ideas were left in the realize the options box for attention later.

On the third AR²T form Stan suggested that we put 'strong financial information systems and controls' into the realize the results box. He asked a fair amount of questions about purchasing limits, key performance indicators (KPIs), how fast Martin got his statements, and how well he understood them. Martin agreed to make that choice even though he didn't understand much about it at the moment. I also specifically included forecast and variance reports at Stan's request.

In the assessment box we put down exactly what Martin said: "I don't really understand bookkeeping. It doesn't make much sense to me. I look at the statements, but they don't help me much."

In the realize the options box Stan suggested that we put down 'creating a forecast of the next twelve monthly statements with benchmarks for the profit centers and introduce key performance indicators'. Martin kind of shrugged and said he was open to learning and that he'd go along. I made myself a note to ask Stan more about key performance indicators later.

The TRaction plan was getting the previous twelve monthly statements from the bookkeeping program, the last two year ends from the accountant, and doing an analysis of the current run rates.

After we left I said to Stan, "Thanks for coming along. We managed to get deeper into it than I've ever been before."

"Not a problem, I really enjoyed it. It appears to me that Martin is a pretty sharp guy who really knows his business inside and out. He just needs to know more about how a strong company is built and he'll be well on his way. My only concern is that he might not find enough time to work on his TRaction plans. He's a pretty busy guy, that phone of his never stops ringing and everybody wants to talk to him. I also noticed that there were no firm dates put onto his TRaction items. That's probably a symptom of how his company operates. When the schedule board is behind I imagine it gets his full attention."

"I know what you mean. I get tired just watching him," I said.

"The collateral value concept and developing a company promise should really help him," Stan said, "but it'll probably take a while for him to wrap his mind around it. I'm sure that his regular clients see Hydro delivering a wider value package than Martin does. I don't think that all his work comes based on price alone. As long as he believes that it does, he'll have a hard time pricing his jobs properly to cover all of his costs and make a reasonable profit. On the other hand, he's looking into the renovation and service markets. If the new construction market won't pay fairly enough for him to earn a profit then shifting the business is a good idea for the company."

"You're right. I never thought of it that way before but you're right on the money there."

We had to hustle to get over to West Valley Auto on time. I was excited about what I learned at our last meeting and curious to see how much of it would apply to Grant's company.

15

We met Grant in the lunch room at West Valley Auto and went through the process again. I felt a lot more confident this time. Stan chipped in here and there, but for the most part he let me lead the discussion.

I described the four bases analogy, telling him how direct costs are first base, overheads are second base, a fair wage for the owner is third base, and profits for the company are home plate where the team scores runs. Grant indicated that he was getting around third most months, home on others, but for a couple months every year he had difficulty even making it to second. Those months were typically in the winter when people have other priorities for their time and money. When the whole year was added together he figured that he was somewhere around third base.

While we were discussing his business model and the value he delivered it became clear that he wanted to run a friendly neighbourhood garage where his customers could drop in and have small repairs done without an appointment. "Stop by anytime and we'll take a look at it," was how he wanted West Valley Auto to operate. That's how he saw his value. I kept digging because it didn't sound like a strong enough company promise to me. Another point that he stressed was good diagnostics. "We identify the parts that are causing the problems and replace only those." He felt that too many of his competitors were what he called 'parts changers'. Replace this one and if that doesn't solve the problem move to the next one and change it too and so on until the problem goes away. Grant believed that this was way too expensive for his customers. West Valley spent a fair amount of time diagnosing to make sure they got it right the first time.

Stan pressed him on the collateral value they delivered and he described a friendly garage where they get to know their clients and take good care of their vehicles. We challenged him to make that into a stronger company promise that resonated with his clients and prospects alike while inspiring his employees.

Next Stan started asking him about profit centers. Grant seemed to know his numbers better than most of the other company owners that I'd talked to. He listed labor, parts, sublet, tires, and shop supplies as his profit centers. He believed that the key profit center was labour. "If you keep the technicians busy working on cars, the parts sell themselves," he said.

I couldn't really keep up with the conversation when Stan and Grant got into how his shop management software worked. Stan was very curious about it.

Then I pulled out the three AR²T forms. As usual it took a bit of time for Grant to get his mind into it. I was really starting to get the sense that most owners didn't think about making choices. After a bit of a discussion regarding the realize the results box, he settled on improving his car count to an average of ten per day. This meant that he wanted to see an extra two customers per day booking their vehicles in for repairs or maintenance. West Valley Auto was currently averaging eight cars per day and we put that into the assessment box.

When it came to filling in the realize the available options box the conversation wandered a bit. Grant talked about the local newspaper advertising he'd been doing, the coupons he'd sent out, and the referral program that he put in place. They didn't seem to be working as well as he wanted them to.

We landed on marketing to the local companies that were close to his location and inviting the people that worked there to have their vehicles serviced during their work hours. Asking for the companies' fleet work went on to the list as well. Grant also talked about how they liked working on recreational vehicles and we figured that it would be a good candidate for a separate AR²T form because there was a lot involved in getting set up to handle a large volume of that type of work.

We also added social media marketing, networking events, sports team sponsorships, neighbourhood flyers, and put a few other ideas to the realize the available options box. I expect other ideas will come to mind as it gets worked on.

For the TRaction plan Grant agreed to design a flyer for the nearby companies and send it to the printers. He also agreed to discuss marketing ideas with his staff and other shop owners he knew. He wanted to limit it to people he didn't compete directly with. Their shops would have to be in other communities.

We started the discussion on the second AR²T form by looking at how well West Valley's profit centers were performing. Labor seemed to be the key. Grant talked about productivity and efficiency ratios. After a few questions I

John Cameron

understood productivity to be the amount of work assigned to each technician in a day. If over the course of an eight hour day a tech was given six hours of work to do, the productivity ratio would be 75%, or six divided by eight. The balance of the time is non-productive. It gets used for tasks like cleaning up, moving vehicles around, waiting for parts to arrive, and an assortment of other things.

Efficiency was how quickly the tech got their assigned work completed. So if a tech was given a six hour job and finished in five hours they would have an efficiency ratio of six divided by five, or 120%. Conversely, if the tech took seven hours their efficiency ratio would be six divided by seven, or 86%.

The results that Grant wanted were a consistent productivity ratio of 85% with an efficiency ratio of 110%. That went into the realize the results box.

When we started to discuss the available options for achieving the results, it became clear that productivity was directly impacted by the car count from the first AR^{2}T form. It wasn't Grant's habit to send people home when the schedule board got light. He really didn't want to start cutting his tech's hours. They had families to feed and mortgages to pay. His service advisor, Steve, had some level of control over productivity based on how he scheduled the flow of cars through the shop, but it mostly boiled down to the amount of incoming calls for appointments.

It also came to light that they spent more time diagnosing than they charged for. This is when they used their most expensive tools. Charging more appropriately would improve both their efficiency and productivity.

A bigger issue around productivity appeared to be recommending work that needed to be done on clients' vehicles. When the car count was high it wasn't a problem because the shop has the productivity hours it needs. When the car count slows down it gets challenging. To get productivity hours the mechanics and the service advisor need to take a good look at every vehicle. They should be inspecting each of them and reviewing their service history to see if anything can be done to prevent future breakdowns or to extend the life of the vehicle's various parts. They should only sell what they know needs to be sold, but by and large they really don't like to sell work. They don't mind fixing the problems or doing the maintenance that customers request but, they feel uncomfortable asking for additional money to do other items. That's even when the technicians know the work needs to be done to maximize the life of their clients' vehicles. This tendency was having a negative effect on West Valley's productivity because there weren't always enough hours for every mechanic every week.

We agreed that auto repair shops have a general reputation for trying to get their customers to overspend. West Valley occupied the other end of the spectrum. They actually erred on the side of under-spending, which had the negative side effect of aging their clients' vehicles faster.

Improving the efficiency, on the other hand, was more straightforward. The techs had different areas of strength. Some were good at diagnostics and slower on repairs. Others were awesome on certain types of repairs, slow on others, and didn't like diagnostics at all. Everyone seemed to do well on the maintenance work like the regular changing of fluids for brakes, steering, and transmissions. Learning from each other was a big topic. There was a healthy discussion and many ideas surfaced.

We went back to the top of the second AR²T form and filled in the assessment box. Grant took a few minutes to calculate that his current productivity ratio was 70% and his current efficiency ratio was 88%. We also noted that they were good at minimizing what the clients spend, which came at the expense of a long, safe life of their clients' vehicles, not to mention West Valley's profitability.

In the realize the results box the targets were 85% for productivity and 110% for efficiency. This meant that the productivity had to rise 15% and efficiency had to go up 22%. I thought that was a lot but Grant said there were shops around that were performing better than that.

I volunteered to summarize the notes from our conversation, put them into the realize the options box and get it back to Grant.

In the TRaction plan Grant asked me to put down 'get better at recommending needed work'. When I pressed him for more detail he added 'regularly reviewing the vehicle inspections and mechanic recommendations to look for opportunities to serve the clients better.'

You can't manage what you don't measure so the productivity and efficiency ratios plus the average dollars per invoice would be reported as KPIs. They would be displayed in the lunch room with daily updates and they would be discussed in detail with the staff every Wednesday during the lunch break.

Steve, the service advisor, should also start asking every client how long they intended to keep their vehicle for. Those that intended to keep them for more than a couple of years should be asked in advance if they wanted to see recommendations that would maximize the life of their vehicle. Then the clients could make their own choices from there. If it was discussed in advance and the clients expected the conversation, it would feel less sleazy and more like the professional service it was.

There was a lot to do on that TRaction plan.

In the realize the results box on West Valley's third AR²T form we put down 'becoming the repair shop of choice for one hundred recreational vehicle owners'. Under assessment Grant thought that they currently took care of about twenty of them.

In the realize the available options box we put 'talking to RV storage places to see if West Valley could put up signage at their locations', 'putting up signage and pictures behind the service counter', 'developing a *bring your RVing friend* referral program', and 'noting the RVs parked outside of homes in the area to prepare for a direct mail campaign'. We also thought that it might be a good idea to talk to the existing RV clients who Grant knew well and ask them for their opinions on how this should be marketed. Advertising RV tune up specials in the winter when the shop was slow seemed to be a good idea. Some retired people head for the sun after Christmas is over.

The TRaction plan was limited to calling five of his existing clients. Grant had his regular work to do plus three AR²T forms in play.

After we finished up, Stan and I went for a quick coffee at the sandwich store at the other end of the complex that West Valley Auto was in. We'd already covered a lot of ground and it wasn't even noon yet. As I sat down I checked my watch it was 11:45. I had forty five minutes before my meeting with Dave from the St. John Pub.

"That was a great meeting. We really got deep into it with Grant," I said as Stan sat down across from me. We had a table for two by the window near the front door. I noticed that in the kitchen they were busy preparing pre-ordered lunches for the workers in the area. It looked like everyone there was getting ready for their daily lunch rush. I made a mental note to tell Grant that it might be a good idea to ask if they would put his flyers into the lunch bags.

"Yeah, he's a pretty sharp guy. How long has he been in business?" Stan asked.

"I think it's been about four years now, but he's worked there longer than that. Grant told me that he and a friend bought West Valley Auto from the previous owner. Then about a year and a half ago his partner wanted out so he bought all the shares."

"I'd really like to see him do well. In fact, I think that I'll start bringing my car there. They seem to know what they're doing and they obviously care about their clients," Stan said.

"He needs to get further around the bases," I suggested.

"Dave always talks about communities needing a good population of companies. It's an interesting viewpoint. After meeting with Martin and Grant I'm starting to see it a little more clearly. They provide jobs and they really want their people to do well. On top of that they want to provide good service to their clients. West Valley needs more people like them to succeed. Their companies are great additions to the community."

"I agree wholeheartedly," I said. "I'm hoping that the whitepaper will make it easier for them and others to build strong companies that serve the community well.

I paused and changed the subject. "How do you think we did filling out the AR²T forms?"

"I think you're off to a pretty good start. It'll be interesting to see how fast they work on their TRaction plans. As they make progress on them and take more time to expand and digest their inventory of options they'll get some good results.

"You almost never get the best ideas right away. On the first pass through the goal is to get some ideas on paper. When we use the AR²T of momentum at Velocity Software we schedule regular meetings to review the AR²T forms. That gives us a chance to work on our TRaction plans and let ideas percolate in our minds. A lot of people I know call this 'drilling into it'. If we're not making the type of progress we want then we get more people involved. We just keep working it until we get the results."

"How long do you think it will take for Grant to see some initial results?" I asked.

"Soon enough, I expect Grant will probably have more time to work on his TRaction plans than Martin will. They are both new to this approach and quite likely they'll need you to hold them accountable. You should follow up with them in a few days to see how they're doing. I'd also suggest that you do some more thinking yourself. You can try asking some of the accountants at your firm for their input as well. I know Dave wants to discuss their AR²T forms at your meeting later today and he'll probably come up with some good ideas for their realize the options boxes. With some TRaction and enough heads in the game, things will start to improve pretty fast."

"On another note," I said, "I find it interesting how sometimes an item from the realize the options box can become an AR²T form all on its own. Like the recreational vehicle servicing from West Valley Auto did."

"It happens. The AR²T Forms are best when they're dialled in to an appropriate level so the TRaction plan items can become doable tasks," Stan replied.

"This has really got my brain working. Boy, has it ever been an interesting day and a half. I feel like I've been riding a roller coaster."

"The learning zone is a lot like that," Stan commented. "Sometimes it seems so close, then just as quickly it can feel like it is a million miles away again. It's challenging to stay balanced as you go through it, especially when there's some pressure on."

I sighed. "Trust me I know all about that. Sometimes that meeting with Mr. Jones is at the top of my mind and I get all anxious Other times I get drawn into the challenges that my clients are facing and finding potential solutions gives me a bit of a high."

"I can see that you really want to help them and you know what? I think you actually are."

"Thanks, I appreciate that."

"Jen, I have to head back to the office now. I've gotten a couple of texts that I need to take care of. When you get to Velocity Software Don't forget to drop by my desk and say hello."

"You can count on that. I really appreciate everything you're doing to help me out."

"It's my pleasure. Have a good meeting over at the pub and stay away from the beer!" Stan said cheerfully. He got up and turned towards the door to leave.

I finished my sandwich and pulled out my AR²T forms for the pub. I tried to imagine what would be on them by the end of the meeting.

16

I pulled into Velocity Software a few minutes early. I'd finished my meeting at the St. John Pub at 1:45 and I planned to arrive at Dave's early because parking was hard to find around there. Velocity Software was over in the industrial part of town in a two building complex. Next door was a freight company, a farm equipment manufacturer was right across the road, and at the far end was a company that manufactured wood trusses for construction projects. All together there were about eight companies in the complex. It seemed to me that Velocity didn't really belong there. I would have thought that Velocity would be more at home in an office building like Carey Jones Norton was.

Stan was up front in the waiting area when I opened the door. He was sitting on one of the comfortable looking couches that were to the right of the reception desk. The hallway that led back to the offices was between the couches and the desk.

"Hi! How was your meeting with Ray?" he asked.

"Hey Stan, it was good, his head cook sat in on the meeting as well. They've got some challenging issues and the AR²T of momentum is helping us to find some solutions. The traffic patterns changed around their location and the revenues are down by about 20%. They need to control costs and do some creative marketing to build the business back up. Ray's thinking about a company promise that will help with that. How've you been?"

"Not too bad at all. Dave's running a few minutes behind and he asked me to give you a quick tour. Let's start with the meeting room."

The meeting room was the first door in the hallway. There was a large poster on the wall that caught my attention.

"That's an interesting poster," I commented. "It doesn't seem to fit around here. Everything appears to happen at a nice even pace. I don't get the sense that you guys are running around putting out fires all the time like some of the companies I've seen."

Stan looked at me with a puzzled expression on his face.

"That's not what it's about," he said as he pointed towards the poster. "The RUN is larger and in the middle because every company should RUN profitably and smoothly deliver on their company promise. That's the main objective. A company is running when it's doing business with clients and handling all of the details that come along with that. It's when they are actively keeping their company promise."

"The key is to understand the words around it. Above the RUN are Design, Build, and Manage. In a perfect world you design the preferred future based on the client's choices, build the software to support it, and then manage the implementation effectively to make sure that it runs the way you planned. We use the poster to keep us on track when we are developing software for our clients. It gets into a bit more in depth, but that's the short version of 'approaching from the North' as we like to call it. When you take that perspective it becomes easier to get the results that everybody wants."

"That's really interesting, I like it."

"Below the RUN are Defend, Blame, and Avoid. If you just look at the first letters they are DBA, which also stands for Doing Business As. Companies sometimes have a number as their legal name like 63262652 Ltd. and then they do business using an operating name. Think of it like AKA, which stands for Also Known As. That's police shorthand for a person using an alias."

"Yeah, I've heard that term before."

"The interesting thing that Dave always points out is that you want to bring your best self to a project not some watered down facsimile of yourself. If you defend the way things are, blame others, or avoid dealing with the issues, then you're not putting your best self forward. In that case you're 'going south' and not really contributing to the success of the project. We call each other on it whenever we see it and we make sure that the clients understand it as well. When they know the difference between approaching from the North and going south it sets the standard for the projects and how everybody interacts. Then nobody loses the focus on creating software that helps the client RUN smoothly and compete more effectively."

As we were about to leave the meeting room Stan stopped, looked back at the poster, and said, "Come to think of it, it reminds me of something Steve Jobs said when he stepped down as Apple's CEO in 2011."

Your time is limited, so don't waste it living someone else's life . . . And most important, have the courage to follow your heart and intuition. They somehow already know what you truly want to become. Everything else is secondary.

Stan went on. "At the time he said that Apple had just become the most valuable publicly traded company in the world, so it's probably good advice."

"Wow, I guess so. Where did the poster come from?"

"I remember Dave saying that it came from his old buddy Mark. He adapted it for software development but I believe that it was originally created for designing and building companies. I know it works very well for software.

If you want to find out more about the business applications you should ask Dave," Stan replied as he motioned towards the door.

"Let's take a look at the bullpen. That's where the programmers set up shop when they're working from here."

We went about thirty feet down the hall and opened a door on the right. We entered a large wide open room with very high ceilings. From the door I could tell that the space was originally designed for industrial use. There was some organization and some randomness to the layout of the desks. One even had a straw umbrella over it. It looked like it had a Hawaiian theme. Some had high tables with tall chairs; others were set up like regular desks complete with bookcases. There were a few round tables with chairs around them. They appeared to be ready for meetings that might happen soon. Down at the end there were four offices with the doors left open. They didn't appear to be assigned to anybody in particular.

"This is kind of neat," I mused.

"It's not for everybody," Stan said. "We've lost some people because they couldn't get used to it. Everyone here knows what they're accountable and responsible for and we're all expected to deliver, but we get to set up how we want, where we want. I like to come in here and work. On the other side of the coin we have a few people who live hundreds of miles away and they only come in six or seven times a year. The rest of the time they telecommute via phone, e-mail, or Skype. It all works out quite well."

Stan introduced me to the six people who were there and they told me about another twenty-five or so employees who were out at client's sites or working from their home offices. There was no way that I was going to keep all of them straight in my mind so I stopped trying and just listened.

Dave strolled into the bullpen and gave us a big wave. "There you are," he called out. "How are you guys doing?"

"Pretty good," we replied in unison.

"Jen, it's great to see you! Thanks for waiting. I had some meetings that ran a little long," Dave said cheerfully. It was good to see him again. I could feel my mood picking up almost instantly.

"No problem," I said. "Stan's been giving me a tour. This place is fascinating. You have no idea what goes on in here when you look at it from the outside."

Dave laughed. "Sometimes you have no idea what goes on in here when you see it from the inside too, but that's okay. We like to challenge our people and see how creative they can get. As long as they're keeping our company promise, it's all good. It can be surprising and good at the same time.

"Speaking of surprises, I hear that you've really jumped in head first. I mean wow, have you ever taken on a lot in the past few days! I can't wait to see the AR²T forms."

"Well, here you go then," I said as I passed over the copies I made for him.

"Let's all sit down and take a look at these," Dave said as he pointed to one of the round tables.

We sat there for a good hour talking about the clients, potential company promises, their AR²T forms, their business models, and where they were on the bases. It was interesting. We, well mostly Dave, came up with some more really good ideas for the realize the options boxes. I wrote them all down. It made me feel more confident about going to the next meetings. We also discussed potential future results that they may want to target and made a list of good questions to ask.

Stan had to get back to work. He headed towards the Hawaiian themed desk. I should have known! Dave spent a few minutes talking about how some of my clients' AR²T forms might be open for a while. That meant it would take some TRaction, more time, and even a few more options that we haven't thought of yet before the results would be realized. He also told me that it wasn't uncommon for AR²T forms at Velocity Software to stay open and active for months.

Dave cautioned me not to champion the new ideas too hard. The clients' choices are a big part of the process. The owner has the right to choose the results they want to pursue and they have the right to choose which items from the realize the available options box they move onto their TRaction plans. He thought my main role was to draw their choices out, make sure they had a healthy inventory of options, and then hold them accountable for their TRaction plans.

He reminded me that it's called the AR²T of momentum for a reason. Beauty is in the eye of the beholder and in this case the beholder is the owner. Dave also cautioned me to be alert for decisions. If an owner says, "I can't do that because . . ." Then they are, in effect, making a decision. It's much better to postpone the decision and run the AR²T of momentum process to see what's really possible.

He also thought that, as they got more experience with the AR²T of momentum, they'd be able to visualize the results they wanted with more clarity. He said they appeared to be making good choices with the information they had, but he felt that it was my role to educate them more about the science side of things: The five key elements for building a strong company.

"Even though we came out of the gate a bit quick, all in all it's a good start," he said.

"Well you said TRaction is good," I replied with a big smile.

He chuckled. "No worries, your clients are further ahead than they were a couple of days ago and you should be proud of that. When they learn more about all five of the key elements they'll make even more progress. So far we've covered the AR²T of momentum and the company promise. The next part of my story with Mark really gets into financial information systems and they're the critical element when it comes to establishing consistent profitability."

"I'm looking forward to it."

"Let's head over to my office," Dave said.

I looked over and waved at Stan as Dave and I left the bullpen.

17

As we settled into Dave's office I said, "Stan's been a big help. Thanks for making him available."

"He's mostly been doing it on his own," Dave replied with a grin. "I don't think he minds helping you out. It appears to me that he's taken a bit of a shine to you. He's been staying late around here to keep up with his work. If I was you I'd pay some attention to him. He's a pretty good guy with a bright future. He'd make a nice catch."

I felt myself going a bit red in the face. I hadn't really thought about Stan that way. I liked him but I'd been too caught up in my own circumstances to really notice him. I didn't know what to say. Thankfully Dave started talking again.

"I'm ready to jump back into the story, but before we get started, do you have any questions?"

"How much time do you have?" I asked with a smile. "Actually I'd like to ask you about the poster that's up on the wall in your meeting room."

"Which poster are you talking about?"

"The one with the big RUN in the middle. Stan told me a bit about it and how you use it nowadays but he said that you and Mark started out using it differently."

"Yeah, that's right. Understanding it will probably help to clear up a few things for you. Did Stan tell you about the DBA?

"Yes he did. It's defend, blame, avoid, or DBA: doing business as a lesser version of yourself. It's going south," I said.

"That's right," Dave replied. "Where do you think Ron from Waltham Signs is headed?"

The light bulb went on for me.

"That pretty much means that he's stuck in the field of complexity," he said. "He can't see his way forward and right now he's probably not coachable. I'm not sure why he agreed to participate in your project. Perhaps he's waiting for you to come in and wave a magic wand that solves his problems."

"I get that sense too." I added.

"Next time you go to see him I'd like to tag along, if you don't mind."

"Thanks, I'd appreciate that."

He continued. "I'd like to know where he wants to see his company five years from now. I suspect that his vision is pretty limited. If hasn't made a choice to pursue a compelling vision then it'll be like trying to work the AR^2T of momentum without filling out the realize the results box."

"I get what you mean. If you don't have anything in the realize the results box then by definition it's impossible to get any TRaction."

"That's right. If Ron sees his company staying pretty much the same place five years from now then there's no call for him to do anything differently," Dave added. "But the competition is going to change and, realistically speaking, staying in the same place is probably going to leave his company high and dry."

"So we need to help him create a vision statement," I said.

"That's a good thought and to really help him we need to carry it a step or two further. We've got to get him believing in a positive future and then we've got to clearly identify the first steps towards it. We need to show him the path and help him get started. Mark did that for me and it made all the difference in the world. If we can't do that for him then we'll just be spinning our wheels without getting any TRaction."

"How do we go about getting him to see a positive future?" I asked.

"First, it will be good to get him working on the AR^2T of momentum using a five year time horizon. That will get him thinking about what he wants out of life, what his goals are for the next five years, and give him someplace to write them down. Under assessment I suspect that he'll have to put down that starting Waltham Signs wasn't really the best idea of his life. If he could go back and unwind it he probably would.

"Where we go from there will be interesting. I'd like to think about it some more, but what comes to mind is asking him what successes he's had in his personal life and his business life. That's the start of an appreciative inquiry. The next step is to bring those positives forward into his future planning.

"I'd also like to ask him what the most successful sign companies are likely to do and to have him ask his suppliers that same question. Just keep digging until we find something that he can work on. He needs to get some wins and then continue to build on them. I'd also like to see him develop good financial information systems starting with a forecast and variance report for the company. That's on my mind because it's coming up next in Velocity Software's story. It helped me to identify what I needed to work on. If he can't see anything getting better it probably won't. It's like a self fulfilling prophecy. We have to turn that around and get him believing that a positive future is possible. That's when he'll be able to make the choices that are best for himself and the company."

"Okay, that sounds like a good plan," I replied.

"If he starts to get some TRaction he should start to break free from the field of complexity, but I suspect that he'll need a lot more direction and encouragement than your other clients."

Dave continued. "At some point I'd like to see you take all of your clients through a five year AR^{2}T of momentum exercise as well. It's important. Done right it should give them all a compelling vision, a motivating destination to work towards, and a plan for building in their company."

"Drawing it out of them is mostly a matter of entertaining the right questions. I can do that," I said.

"That's a good example of appreciative inquiry right there. Your journalism skills can be brought forward and applied to a new challenge, this gives you the confidence you'll need to be successful. That's stepping into your learning zone with one foot still in your comfort zone. That's a good approach to growth of any kind," he said.

"I see what you mean and it makes sense," I responded.

"Your clients may or may not have thought five years out before. You really want each of them to get a clear picture of what they want their company and their life to be like. Some questions to consider might be: What will your role in the company be like? How many hours will you be working? How many holidays will you be taking? What stature in the industry will your company hold? What products and or services do you expect the company to be selling? How profitable will it be? What will the revenues be? What company promises will you be making and keeping? What assets will you personally have? What type of physical shape will you be in? You can probably come up with some other questions that will help them get a really good visualization."

"I'm sure that I can help them with that," I said.

"Great. I know from personal experience that holding a vision actually changes the way that you approach difficulties. Problems seem smaller and not as serious. You walk with more confidence and that helps to attract the type of business you want. Everything gets easier when you see yourself in the early stages of a journey that you fully expect to be successful on. I was really lucky when Mark drew out my vision, helped me to make my choices, and instilled me with confidence.

"That's awesome," I said.

"It's more important than most people think," Dave replied. "It doesn't have to take very long and it makes a big impact."

He paused again and started looking around his office at the pictures on the wall.

After a couple of minutes he continued. "It should also give them a sense of the body of work that will be involved with their company over the next five years. In some respects it's more than most people imagine, in other respects it's less. In my mind I like to divide the work into two categories. The first category is the work that goes into developing the company and the second category is the work involved in processing the business"

"Wouldn't you say the first category is the design, build, and manage part and the second category is the running or doing business part?" I chipped in.

"You're right," Dave replied, "It pays to focus on the first part. When you've built a strong company the business flows with less effort. For example, the time that it takes to develop accountability and build systems is small in comparison to the amount of time it takes to run without systems in place, especially when the company has to bring new employees on.

"It's important for owners to realize that building the strength of the company makes processing the business easier. For example, think about how many times Grant's company is going to prepare work orders. With a car count of ten per day, that's 50 per week and then there are 52 weeks in a year. Less the holidays, that comes to about 2,590 per year and over five years it'll be 12,950 times. That's just one example. There are a lot of things that are going to happen 12,950 times as his company processes the business. They'll all need to be done consistently well for Grant to achieve his goals. Come to think of it, that's also how many times West Valley is going to have to keep their company promise to their clients."

"Wow, that's a lot."

"It just makes sense to start looking at these things. When the business RUNs there are some moving parts with a lot of RPMs and they need lubrication, to use an engine analogy. These are prime candidates for systemization and it makes sense to ask whether the systems should be developed now or whether he should wait until later, say after year five. It's the sooner the better, in my humble opinion."

I chipped in again. "I can see what you're talking about here. The first part is to draw out the five year design and then it becomes easier to see what systems need to be built into the company and why."

"That's right. Approaching from the North using the design build approach always makes things easier. Your clients appear to be trying to work from RUN up. They're running uphill and that's quite a bit more challenging, but it's also not all that unusual for companies at the stage of growth you've chosen to write about for your whitepaper."

"I know what you mean," I said. "I wish I was doing a better job for the clients."

"Don't be too hard on yourself. You started by using the AR²T of momentum to work on your clients' current symptoms, issues, and problems. That's okay. That's what's real for them right now and getting some TRaction will give them a sense that they're moving forward. Fairly soon though, you should be stretching their vision farther out into the future and work towards developing a design build approach," he said.

"That makes a lot of sense."

"They may give you some pushback by saying that it's planning and things have hardly ever worked out like they planned in the past and that's probably true for them. There's an old military saying:

No plan survives contact with the enemy.

That's why the AR²T of momentum is an ongoing dynamic process that focuses on the results."

I nodded. Dave had a way of explaining everything so clearly.

"Alright then," Dave said. "Can I pick up where we left off on the story about how Mark helped me introduce the Company Strength Program into Velocity Software?"

"Sure," I replied, remembering how much I'd been looking forward to it.

PART FOUR

As Told by Dave

18

"Dave, how are you doing?" Mark asked me as he walked into Velocity's old offices on Third Avenue at about 7:45 AM.

"Not bad," I answered. I remember that I was actually feeling hopeful for a change.

"Well Dave, let's get to work then," Mark said with a smile as he reached out to shake my hand. It was a good solid handshake but somehow it seemed uncomfortable to me. Lately the strong people that I'd been dealing with had been running right over me.

"Would you like a coffee?" I asked.

"That'd be great," Mark replied. We walked down towards the coffee room that wasn't really a room. It was just an open closet-shaped space off the main hallway with a small sink built into a counter. It had cupboards above and below. I wasn't sure what to say to him. I looked over at Mark and was impressed by how he carried himself in a friendly, confident way.

Patrick was always the first one into work in the mornings. He'd already made a fresh pot of coffee a few minutes earlier. Mark cut into the silence as I opened the top cupboard and reached for two mugs.

"I'd like to be clear on something. There's an important attribute to coaching. Think about softball for a bit. When I'm coaching softball I can't go on the field when the games are being played. I can give guidance and feedback from the dugout or the coach's box. I can even call in a few plays but the kids have to play the game on their own, for the most part."

"That's right," I said, wondering where he was going with this.

"Where I have the biggest impact is at the practices," Mark went on. "That's when I'm actually on the field with the players. I set out the practice plans. The key is to get them doing things that they wouldn't otherwise do, all with the aim of improving their attitudes, skills, and knowledge, which in turn leads to improved performance in games. If I showed up at a practice and just dropped off the equipment bag pretty soon a game of scrub would break out. The kids would play and sure they would get better over time from just playing, but there is no way that they would improve as much as they will with structured practices."

"That's right," I said again, feeling a bit foolish about not having something more intelligent to contribute to the conversation.

Mark didn't seem to mind. "Today we're going to work on developing a forecast and variance report. You were saying last night that you haven't done one before," he paused. "It's the central piece in a good financial information system. It's all about how money flows through your company.

"I'll tell you right out of the gate that this is the number one activity for establishing consistent profitability. The other thing that you should know in advance is that the first time you do pretty much anything you're not likely to be much good at it. It'll frustrate you and your bookkeeper for a while, but then in a couple of months it'll be simple and you'll both be wondering how you ever ran this company without it."

"I thought that you were coming to take a look and see if the company is worth saving," I said.

"That's right," he said in his friendly manner. "Based on our conversation last night at the Diamond I suspect that it is. The only way we'll know for sure is to put together a realistic forecast of the next year's profits and we'll do that by creating your next twelve monthly income statements before they happen."

"You make it sound so easy. I'm not so sure."

"Well, we'll have to take a look at the balance sheet too, but if I remember correctly you're up to date with your payroll, government payments, and bank loans. That's a good thing. I'm interested to see how far behind you are on your supplier payables though," Mark said.

I looked around to make sure nobody was listening in. "We've been stretching them as far we can. Some are current because they stay right on top of us and others are a few weeks behind. It's funny, the nicer people are to us the more we stretch them out." I hung my head before I caught myself and looked back at Mark. I looked him in the eyes and for a brief instant I wondered if I should be doing that. It really made me feel awkward having somebody come in to help me.

"Don't worry too much about that right now. You're not the only one who's ever gotten behind on the bills. It's good that you're keeping the important ones up to date. From what I can tell, nobody's going to come in and shut you down anytime soon."

Mark put his hand on my shoulder. Somehow he had a way of making me feel better. It was as if he was passing some of his positive energy on to me.

"So, where are we going to set up and get to work?" Mark asked.

"Carol does the bookkeeping on her computer up at the front. She'll be here in a few minutes."

"Okay, to get started we'll need the last two year-ends from your accountant and the last twelve monthly income statements from her. Then we'll be able to get an idea about the current run rates."

"Current run rates?" I asked.

"An example of that would be to look at your custom software sales for the past couple of years and see if they are staying level or trending up or down. If, say, they are steadily increasing by 10% year over year then we can comfortably predict that they will be up 10% again next year. We'll do this for all of your accounts; expenses included, and use the run rates to make our initial forecast for next year."

"That makes sense."

"Next I'll ask if there are any expected changes on the horizon that need to be incorporated. These could be raises that you've promised your employees, an increase coming in your rent, perhaps accounting for rising fuel costs, and such. It could even be some new business that you're sure is headed your way."

"It sounds like a bit of work."

"It's like anything else Dave, it takes time to learn but eventually it'll become second nature. It seems complex now but put some time into it and you'll understand it soon enough, then it'll be simple and you won't be able to unlearn it.

"A forecast is a numerical representation of your business model for the next year. If you don't like what you see, then we'll need to identify the changes that have to be made to get you the profits you deserve."

"I'm pretty sure that something has to change," I said. "It can't keep going the way it has."

"We'll figure it out. From what you told me last night at the Diamond Café it appears that you have three profit centers: your proprietary software, writing custom software, and your field technicians. It will be interesting to see what their margins are running at."

"That might be harder to figure out than you think. We don't separate things out that way in the bookkeeping," I replied.

"I'm not really surprised by that," he said with a bit of a chuckle. "Don't get worried about it though. Almost every small company I've ever worked with doesn't have a well thought-out chart of accounts."

"Chart of accounts?" I said out loud before I could even think about it. Mark took it as an opportunity to explain.

"Your chart of accounts is the foundation of your bookkeeping system. It sets out how everything gets tracked and recorded. In theory you can have as many accounts in your bookkeeping system as you want. By and large most companies don't have enough. For example, instead of putting everything into one big revenue account, each one of your profit centers should have its own unique revenue account. Don't worry, they can still be added together to show your total revenue.

"Your direct costs, which are also known as the cost of goods sold, take their lead from the revenue accounts. They are the other halves of the profit centers. All of the direct cost accounts that are associated with each of the profit centers should be grouped together and totaled. This way the performance of your profit centers becomes easy to see. Then they all add together to show your total direct expenses, total gross profit, and the gross margin."

"I'm following you," I said.

"The overhead expenses, which are also sometimes known as general, sales, and administrative expenses, should be split into cost centers that way you can tell how much it's costing you to keep the different parts of the company running."

"That sounds like it could be a lot of work Mark."

"It can be done. Think about it from the other side: if it's not done, you'll continue working hard for no profits."

I didn't say anything.

"The challenging part is going to be the account numbers. Every account has a name and a number. The accounting software wants to put all the accounts into numerical order. I'm pretty sure the numbers that you currently have in your chart of accounts aren't going to line up your accounts in a way that effectively shows your profit centers and cost centers. We'll probably have to build a spreadsheet and transfer the data. We can rework the account numbers at your fiscal year-end. **It's really not a good idea to change the numbers on your chart of accounts during the middle of a fiscal year**. Before you make the changes you should let the accountant, who does your year-ends, clearly know what you're doing and why you're doing it."

"This is getting a bit complicated," I said.

"It's worth the effort. Accountants want to boil income statements down to one page. That process refines useful management information right out of the statements. I mean, when you look at your monthly statements, can you tell how profitable your field techs are?"

"Not really, all I can do is guess at it."

"Do you want to know?"

"Yes of course. I'd also like to know how the programming is doing and if my own software is profitable or not."

"Your statements are dangerously close to being trivia. We'll work towards setting them up so they become part of a good financial information system. The difference between the two is that information supports the choices and decisions you need to make and trivia doesn't.

"Let me put it this way: you and Carol already enter most all of the data from your source documents. For example, every invoice coming or going contains data, your quotes contain data, your timecards contain data, and your bank statements contain data. You're already entering almost all of the data. We'll probably need some more detail but, I don't think you'll need to enter much more data. This is not about creating more work. The problem is that your financial information systems currently don't process your data into the information you need to see."

I felt pretty inadequate at this point. I sighed and said, "I don't know why I ever got started in this business."

"Hey, get your chin up. You're not the only one. This is a disease of epidemic proportions in the business world, especially for the owners of small to medium sized companies. I say dis-ease because it's certainly not easy to run a company with poor information.

"We're going to take some pretty good steps in the right direction here today. I'm not trying to criticize you. This is just one of my pet peeves. It bugs me how many people just like you get into trouble because they don't get the information they need to run their companies. The accounting rules were designed to serve the taxman, the banks, and investors in public companies. It's clear to me that the accounting industry hasn't put enough emphasis on the needs of small company owners like you."

Carol came through the door. I said good morning to her and introduced her to Mark. I was amazed at how he greeted her like she was a long lost friend. He seemed to be able to develop a rapport instantly with most everybody he met.

While Carol was getting settled in for the day, Mark turned to me and continued. "You know, if your financials had been giving you good information that was well organized then I'm pretty sure you would've taken corrective action long before you got into this much trouble."

"That's an interesting perspective," I said.

"Sorry I got off on one of my rants, but it's something that I firmly believe in. Has your accountant or anybody ever asked you what information you need to run your company?"

"No."

"Do you get any information from your statements that you use to make choices and decisions?"

"No."

"Well, I want you to think about the information you need. Then I'm going to help you set up a financial information system that processes your data into useful information. It's been my experience that when company owners get the right information they almost always make good choices and decisions. Today we're going to set up your bookkeeping with profit centers and cost centers. From there we are going to project your next twelve income statements based on the current run rates and then we'll discuss the changes you need to make in the company in order to get the type of results you want. At the end of the process we'll have a numerical representation of your business model and a list of things that need to be worked on."

It took a while but over the course of the day we set up for the three profit centers: proprietary software, custom programming, field tech services, and I added a fourth for hardware sales. I also asked for five overhead cost centers: facility expenses, vehicle expenses, sales and marketing expenses, financial expenses, and management and admin expenses, which would include a fair wage for me.

The process was interesting. We wound up adding about fifteen new accounts to the chart of accounts. Like Dave suggested it did have to be transferred to a spreadsheet. Carol suggested that we send a copy of the spreadsheet to the accountant so he would know what we were working on. She also thought it would be worthwhile to ask him for his comments. That way we could be sure that he reviewed it. Dave thought it was a **great idea**. Accountants are familiar with the regulations and **they should be consulted**.

The forecast was set up with a revenue line for each of the profit centers at the top. Then the total revenue was calculated. Below the revenues section was the direct cost section. Each of the four profit centers had their associated direct costs grouped together and neatly added up. I could easily see the margins for every profit center. Below the direct cost section was a line that calculated the total direct cost for the entire operation. Then the overall gross profit for the whole company was totaled and on the line below that the gross margin percentage was shown.

This was followed by the five cost centers. Each one of them had a number of accounts in them. They're sometimes called line items. My facility expenses included rent, utilities, maintenance, insurance, telephone, and Internet as line items. The cost for each line item was shown in dollars and on the line just below that it was also displayed as a percentage of the revenue. Each cost center was totaled and also shown in terms of dollars and shown as percentage of revenues. I could see right away that the cost center part of the report was going to be a valuable tool when it came to controlling costs.

Then all the cost centers were neatly added together and the bottom line profit was calculated.

It took a while to uncover the current run rates we needed for the forecast. Often we had to go into the accounting software and print out the accounts to see what had been entered into them. Sometimes we even had to dig a little further and find the invoices to see what they were actually for. It was a real learning experience.

When the forecast was finished we sat down at my desk and Mark showed me how to read the spreadsheet. "The key is to think in terms of a dollar. When you get a dollar of revenues in for software development sixty cents goes directly into your programming costs. That's first base. You have forty cents left, that's your gross margin. The cost center percentages on the spreadsheet also read like cents on the dollar. Four point six cents of every dollar goes to cover the cost of your facility expenses. Two point six cents goes towards your vehicle expenses. Eight cents goes into sales and marketing, which includes your sales rep's wages. Four point five cents goes towards financial expenses. Finally, twenty point one cents of every dollar is spent on management and admin expenses which includes your salary. When you get to the bottom there is nothing left."

"I could have told you that," I said with a laugh.

"It's good to see that you haven't lost your sense of humor, but hey, you don't have even one of your profit centers over 40% and your overheads including wages are a bit over 40%. The business model isn't working. You're not quite making it to third."

"Yeah, I know," I said. "I haven't taken my full pay for quite a while now."

"Well Dave, now for the good news. You're going to learn from your history, but you aren't going to re-live it. It's time to create another forecast spreadsheet and change the numbers a bit based on some realistic improvements that you think can be made. The idea is to create a profitable company on paper first and then get to work and make it happen in the real world."

"Okay, I'm looking forward to that."

"Then every month we're going to compare the forecast to the actual numbers as they come in and see where the variances are. If they're better that'll be great, if they're worse then we'll know where we need to get in and manage. I think a part of your problem was that your business model was based on some assumptions. You didn't have strong enough financial information systems in place to get you the right feedback and see if they held up in the real world."

"I really like how this presents the numbers. It's so much easier for me to understand," I said. "Do forecast and variance reports always look like this?"

"No not always. We created your profit centers based on the way you think about your company. There are lots of options other companies use sometimes, like customer segments, geography, products and services, and locations if a company has multiple facilities for example. It really depends on what makes sense for the owner. The idea is to come up with a format that matches the business model and how the owner thinks about the company. That way it becomes easier to identify areas where improvements can be made. I think that I see some now."

"What do you see?" I asked.

"Like I thought, your company is not fully rewarding you for the time and effort you're putting in but it's not going under either. In my opinion, this thing is going to continue to be somewhat of a black hole in your life until the performance of the profit centers improves. I'd like you to pick one to start with, then we'll adjust the forecast and I'll help you get the results you want."

"Sounds good," I said.

"I'll see you at the game tonight. I'm looking forward to starting Ann at first base. She's really picking the position up fast. I think she's a natural there."

"She sure seems to enjoy it," I said, and then I added, "Maybe the team can teach me a thing or two about rounding the bases!"

19

Ann's game didn't start until 7:30. I went to the park right after supper to help Teru on the batting cage for an hour or so. It never occurred to me to call Teru beforehand; instinctively I knew he'd be there. Sure enough, he was busy cutting the wood to button up the forms. The rebar had already been installed by a contractor. A couple of volunteer dads were hammering in the pieces as he was running the saw.

"The footings look good," I commented as I walked up. "Can I give you a hand?"

"Thanks Dave, that would be great," he said, motioning for me to carry some plywood over to the saw horses.

We made small talk for a few minutes as we took turns marking and cutting lumber. "How's it going with Mark?" Teru asked.

"Pretty good so far, he's helped me with some of the groundwork in bookkeeping and financial information systems that I needed to get into place. We're creating a forecast and we've talked about the purpose Velocity Software is designed to serve, or more accurately should be designed to serve. It's all about the value that I'd like Velocity Software to deliver and to whom. We're working on a company promise that reflects that. I need to come up with one that is compelling to my target market and inspiring to my employees."

"Good stuff," Teru said, "any thoughts so far?"

"It's early," I replied. "It's only been two days but I certainly feel better about things."

"And how about your staff, are they inspired yet?" Teru asked.

"They're basically the same," I admitted. "I guess I need to find a better way to include them in the process, even at this early stage. Do you have any ideas on how?"

Teru thought for a moment. "Yeah, I think I do." In what I quickly discovered to be 'true Teru fashion,' he put the lumber down and told me a story. Naturally, I was riveted.

"In ancient times a great king had ordered the construction of an ornate temple. One day he disguised himself, left his palace, and went to the temple work site to see the progress was being made. The king happened upon one of his workers. 'What are you doing?' he asked.

"The worker didn't recognize the king. 'What does it look like I'm doing?' he snapped. 'I've got these rotten tools, this useless chisel, a stupid hammer, and I'm cracking rocks all day. My back is always sore and my feet hurt constantly. I don't get paid nearly enough for this nonsense.' The worker clearly wasn't happy.

"The king, startled, moved to a different part of the site where another man was working. 'What are you doing?' he asked again.

"The second worker started speaking before he looked over towards him, 'I'm working hard to shape these stones just the way the foreman wants them. Then they'll all fit together nicely and form a piece of the building. I'm taking pride in doing it right.' The king smiled and nodded. That was more like it.

"The king moved on again and found a third man. 'What are you doing?' he asked.

"The worker's face lit up into a big smile. 'Can't you tell?' he asked without expecting an answer. 'I'm building a cathedral! It's going to be beautiful, full of marble, gold, and silver. If we work hard enough, it might be ready in time for my children to worship in it. Think of all the weddings and the ceremonies that will take place inside. It's going to be the heart of the community. People are going to celebrate the big moments of their lives here.' The king was very impressed.

"You see Dave, all three workers were doing exactly the same thing, but they had different ways of relating to their work. It all comes back to how they connect to the overall purpose. The more you can focus your team on your company's purpose, the more successful you'll all be. I think that's what Mark calls delivering on the company promise."

Thirty feet away, two of the baseball dads grunted and groaned as they pushed some wood up into place. Teru looked over and instantly diagnosed the opportunity for me to experience the lesson first hand.

We walked around the far side to one of the dads. "How's it going?" Teru asked.

"Not great," he replied. "The forms aren't fitting quite right and we're wasting time doing this. We should just hire some professionals and be done with it."

We let a minute or two go by and then went over to another one of the volunteer dads. "How's it going?" Teru asked again.

"Not bad at all," he said. "I think we'll have the forms ready in a couple of hours. I'm working to get them perfectly straight. We won't be able to change it once the concrete is poured. If the foundation is crooked, think of what will happen to the brick walls. I'm taking pride in doing it right."

Teru and I walked back toward the saw.

"There's only one problem with the lesson," I said. "We don't have the third guy over there."

"Dave," he laughed, "I'm the third guy. I come here and work on this batting cage almost every day for one reason: the kids. I think about them learning to bat better and the confidence that will come along with that. Some of them have real potential to do something special on the field. This batting cage is going to help us hone their skills faster. Their confidence is going to soar and they'll carry that over into other parts of their lives. This isn't just a batting cage. It's a testament to our league's slogan: Everybody Wins."

"I get it now but how does it apply to business?" I asked.

"Well," Teru said, "you've got to consistently reinforce the purpose of the company to your people. It takes more repetition than you think. There's a reason why I can't really do it here. Most of the volunteers only put in a few hours here and there. Not to mention, some of them only show up because their wives make them," he laughed again.

"You know, thinking of your company again. Your employees are much more likely to work hard to serve the company promise than they are to work hard just make you some money. Never forget that. You really have to define your company promise and reinforce it again and again."

From across the field I could hear the crowd at the team's first exhibition game of the season singing the national anthem.

"Enjoy the game," Teru said. "Mark tells me he thinks Ann is set for a big year."

"I think she is too," I replied. "Will you be here after the game? I'd like to introduce you to my wife."

"You know me," Teru smiled. "I'm almost always here."

20

Ann's team played well, hustling on every pitch, and coming out with a nine—four win. It was remarkable to see that many twelve year olds focused on one thing for an hour and a half.

Ann went three for four at the plate, with two runs batted in. Her batting had certainly improved since last year. But more important was her attitude. She was continually smiling, slapping teammates on the back, and offering encouragement. I couldn't help but notice that the team was beginning to take on the character of their coach, Mark. Perhaps there was a lesson there.

The nice thing about watching softball is that it gives you plenty of time to think. I pondered Velocity Software's purpose and wondered what the company promise should be as Mark and Teru had been challenging me to do. If I'm going to devote that much of my life to building an organization, just what is the value that I wanted it to deliver? What should the body of work look like when I'm done?

I kept coming back to that night when I had the breakthrough and told Karen about my idea.

My words to her that night rolled around and around in my mind. "I've been playing around with some program code," I said, "and I think I've found a way to do enterprise resource planning on a smaller scale so any small business anywhere could use it. It's simple. I can't believe it's not being done already. I can do this thing, Karen. It's a million dollar idea. It'll help a lot of small companies that are struggling to compete with importers and larger companies who can afford to have computer programmers on staff."

Every time I strayed from the simplicity and beauty of my original purpose—technology that helps smaller companies compete and win—I felt overwhelmed. But when I stuck to it, I flourished. I started thinking through the list of Velocity's clients with that in mind and a stream of good business ideas started to flow. It felt good to feel my curiosity awakened in a positive way again.

"That's it," I mumbled aloud to no one in particular during the fourth inning. "We develop technology that helps smaller companies compete and win." The field of IT is expanding rapidly and most small organizations can't afford an in house IT department. Heck, at Velocity Software we've got a team of professionals and even we have trouble keeping up with the pace of new technology. Most companies are completely busy just doing their day to day business. They just don't have the time or energy to devote to their IT, let alone take the time to understand how it can help them compete.

After the game, I took Karen over to meet Teru. They hit it off instantly of course as they found common ground in their enjoyment of teasing me. I didn't mind; it was good to see Karen laugh. We hadn't been doing much of that over the past few months.

As we began to leave, Teru stopped us.

"So Karen, I'd like to ask you a favor."

"Sure," she answered.

"Can I borrow Dave on Saturday morning?"

"Absolutely, keep him as long as you want." They both had a good laugh.

"Where are we going?" I asked Teru.

"First we're going for breakfast and then we're heading back here to the batting cage. The cement for the foundation walls is coming and I've only got the pumper truck donated for four hours so we're really going to have to hustle to get all the cement poured."

"You're about to meet up with the best bunch of guys you could ever hope to cross paths with," Teru said. "Just be at the Diamond Café at 7:30 Saturday morning."

"Nice to meet you Karen, see you Saturday Dave." He waved and went back to work.

21

When I arrived at the café just before 7:30, Teru was already there unlocking the door.

"Do you own this place?" I asked, forgetting for a moment that Mark had told me about Doug the owner a few days before.

"No," Teru said, "but I've known Doug for a long time. He doesn't open until eight on Saturdays, so he gave me a key to let the Breakfast Boys in."

Teru let me in, turned on the lights, and started fiddling with a coffee maker. He obviously felt very comfortable in the Diamond. After a few moments, he slid a few tables together in the right field section and invited me to sit down across from him.

"So who comes to these breakfasts?" I asked.

"Well, there are the regulars: Mark of course, and a bunch of other people who've either coached or umpired in the West Valley Softball League. Today we've got a few extra people coming. We need some more strong backs to get the cement poured."

"Wow, do you guys get together every Saturday?"

"Yeah, it's a bit of a tradition. We get a few things done, but ninety percent of the time it's just for the sake of shooting the breeze," Teru answered. "Most of their kids have grown up and moved on. Now they sponsor teams, a few still coach, and others do some umping, but best of all they help to train the new coaches and umps," he said with a smile.

Over the next twenty to thirty minutes the other Breakfast Boys, as Teru called them, arrived. To a man they were friendly and curious, which was par for the course at the Diamond Café. They asked me some questions about my life, my company, and of course how Ann's team was doing. A few of them even knew her and remarked about how good of a kid she was.

I really enjoyed the atmosphere at breakfast. There was a lot of laughter, lots of stories, some good natured needling of politicians and lawyers, and even a classic impression of Mark by Teru.

I had a great conversation with Phil Orman who sat next to me. Phil was the assistant coach on Ann's team. He asked me how it was going with Mark and he went on to tell me how Mark helped him design and build his painting company that he sold a couple of years back when he retired.

We talked about purpose and he mentioned that Mark would be asking me not just about the public purpose of the company, which is the company promise, but also about the private purpose of the company in terms of my life. Building a company is a large, complex project to take on. What purpose did I want it to serve in my life? What did I want to get out of it?

Phil explained that his painting company had given him the type of work he enjoyed doing, which was designing, building, and managing a company in the painting business. He loved the industry but said he didn't need to be on the painting tools at all for his last fifteen years in business. The company provided him a good income to raise his family. That included a nice house, lots of vacations, university educations, and weddings for his girls. To top it off he got a nice retirement fund from the sale of the company. That was combined with an ongoing income stream because he continued to own the building that his old painting company still occupies. He got everything he wanted from his company.

Phil and I also talked about how people make choices about the hours they want to put into their companies. When he was working he didn't mind putting in regular hours, although he did admit that he had more freedom to take time off than most people did. Other owners want to design and build companies that run without them. It's possible he said, but that wasn't his style.

Teru had been listening in on our conversation and he cut in with a typical Teru story.

"One day in Ireland three tourists rented a car and spent the day driving and sightseeing through the lush green country side. Late in the day, after taking in the sights, the tourists became lost. Up ahead on the road they spotted a farmer leaning on a fence, they stopped and asked for directions.

'If you were going to Dublin from here, which way would you go?'

'Well', the farmer replied, 'if I was going to Dublin, I wouldn't start from here!'

It begs the question: where would you start from?" Teru added.

Phil jumped back in. "In business, start with the value you want to deliver, which is your company promise. The more value you deliver, the more value you should get in return. Remember, I'm talking both direct and collateral value for everybody here. Then you have to design the business model and the company to deliver for all concerned. If you're like most people you'll have to start at a manageable size and keep building from there. As long as you stay profitable, you'll be able to keep your company in the game."

"You know Phil, I wasn't finished with my story yet. Do you mind?" Teru asked cheekily.

Phil laughed. "No, go right ahead."

"Well, the three sightseeing tourists didn't like the farmer's answer and they drove away, eventually getting even more lost. As it was getting dark they spotted an inn and pulled in. They asked if they could stay for the night. The desk clerk checked and remarked that he only had one room left. The tourists then asked if they could pay with American money. The clerk looked up the conversion rate and told them it was $30.00. They each pulled out a $10.00 bill, paid the clerk, and headed up to the room."

"A while later the desk clerk realized that he'd done the conversion wrong. The room should have only cost $25.00. He called over the Bellboy and gave him five one dollar bills to take up to the tourists' room."

"The tourists realized that they couldn't divide the five dollars equally by three so they each took a $1.00 bill and tipped the bellboy $2.00.

Now each of the three guests has paid $9.00 and three times nine equals $27.00.

The Bellboy has $2.00. His $2.00 plus the tourist's $27.00 equals $29.00, not the $30.00 they initially paid.

Where did the other Dollar go?" Teru asked.

I couldn't figure it out for the life of me. Phil had a big grin on his face. Teru had already moved on to another conversation with somebody else. There were so many conversations going on around the table it was impossible to keep up with them all.

"I'd tell you the answer, but Teru might get mad at me," Phil said. "I think he's showing this to you so you can see how a problem can seem unsolvable one minute and then easy the next. Once you see the solution to the problem it will never fool you again. I think your challenges with the company are going to turn out the same way and I suspect that for you, the farmer on the side of the road is Mark; if you listen to him you won't get lost. At least that's the way it was for me."

"That's pretty good, Phil," Teru said as he turned back towards us. "I like it. When you're struggling with a problem it can be hard to recognize the way forward. The solutions can be easy to miss. That's when it's good to get some advice, but that's not why I told the story.

"For me the neat thing about this story is that the vanishing dollar represents the profit that often goes missing when company owners get too focused on making money for themselves and they lose sight of delivering value. Almost inevitably this makes it more difficult for the company to establish consistent profitability. True long term success in business comes when owners see a connection between the value their company delivers and the rewards they expect to receive."

"It also works the other way around as a lesson for people who don't recognize the full value they deliver and then they price themselves too low to make a profit. I mean the Inn gave a pretty big discount there and they didn't have too," Phil said.

"Either way profits can vanish pretty quickly," Teru said. "And that's the point of the story. Mark knows how to sort that stuff out."

On that note I got up and went towards the cash register at home plate to pay for my bacon and eggs.

Teru called out, "You're too late!"

"What's that?" I said.

"Bruce already got the bill."

I found out that each week somebody picked up the whole tab for everybody. It was a bit of a competition to get your credit card to Julie before anybody else did.

As we left Phil walked to the door with me. When we were out of Teru's earshot he said, "The dollar isn't missing. The front desk has twenty five, the bellboy has two, and the three tourists have one each. That makes thirty."

"Really," I said. "What happened then? Why did it seem like a dollar was missing?"

Phil got a big smile on his face. "The way Teru tells the story he deliberately breaks a rule of mathematics and it's really hard to notice. Heck, I'm not even sure what rule he breaks, but it has to do with mixing addition and multiplication. Stick with the adding and it works out no problem.

"On the other hand," he continued as walked to our cars, "I'll leave you with something else to think about," he said as he handed me a piece of paper. "Business-people try to break the laws of mathematics."

When I got into my car I looked at what he'd written.

A business-person's objective is to make

1+2+3 =123

A business opportunity

+

Invested Resources

+

Their time

=

A Profitable and Successful Company

A great company is worth more
than the sum of the parts that created it

22

As I pulled into the parking lot at West Valley Park the pumper truck was in place. Its boom was already stretched out high into the sky over the work site. The first cement truck was just arriving. It was a nice spring morning. The sun was shining and I remember thinking that it was good to be doing something other than business.

The Breakfast Boys were all finding their parking spots. It looked like we were going to have about ten volunteers. I didn't have any idea about how I fit into the work plan for the day.

Mark called out, "Hey Dave, wait up."

He jumped out of his truck and jogged over, "It's a good thing that we've got a lot of help. Even with that I think that we're going to be sore and tired by this afternoon.

I asked Teru to pair us together so we can talk about your business model and forecast."

Just then I heard Teru yell, "Alright, everybody in. We've got a lot of work to do and I'll give you the rundown about how it's going to go. We are going to start the concrete pour on the south end. It's the shortest wall and then we are going to work down towards the high walls over here on the north end."

He handed out the work pretty quickly. Two people were assigned to the hose from the pumper truck. I was glad that it wasn't me. To get cement into the walls on the north end they would have to stand on top of twelve foot high forms and move the pumper truck's hose at the same time.

Two others were given the task of working the two cement vibrators, one on the west side and the other on the east. Their job was to drop the vibrators into the forms and make sure that the cement settled evenly right down to the bottom. It appeared to me that they would have to stand on top of the forms as well.

Teru called on Mark and I to be one of the two teams working the trowels. Thankfully we could work off of ladders when walls got high at the north end. Our job was to make sure the top of the cement was level and smooth. We were told to be careful to keep the cement even with the bright blue lines that Teru had already put inside the forms.

The last two people were assigned the role of relief helpers. Their job was to keep an eye on everybody and jump in when somebody needed a break.

The footings appeared to be a big rectangle with an extra wall going across in the middle about twenty five feet from the north end. I asked Mark what the extra wall was for and he explained to me that the batting cage was going to be in the south end of the building and the north end would be two stories with storage for the tractor and field supplies on the bottom floor and the equipment and uniform storage on the top floor.

It was painstaking work. The top of the cement was about a foot below the top of the six inch wide forms and there was rebar sticking up at regular intervals. We had to stick our trowels in there and level it off. Sometimes we had to scoop out extra cement because it was too high and other times we had to bring some more in to get the cement up to the level line.

After we got settled into a routine Mark asked me, "So what do you think about the forecast for Velocity Software given the current run rates?"

"I'm not happy about it," I replied. "If everything stays on the same track it looks like I'll be working all year to make a salary of $24,000. I'd probably make more than that if I worked the same amount of hours flipping burgers at McDonalds."

"So what do think the solution is?"

"I was hoping that you were going to tell me," I said.

Mark chuckled. "At our last meeting I asked you to think it over. I've got some ideas but first I'd like to hear what you think."

"Well, like you said none of my profit centers are performing like they should. I'm thinking that we should start with the field techs. The new reports showed me how poorly that profit center was performing. I didn't realize it was that bad before. I think it's the place to start. The 32% in unbilled time really surprised me. I knew that a fair amount of time didn't get billed out but I didn't realize that it was that far out of control.

"We're not far off with hardware sales with an 8% margin. There we only expect 10% to start with. There's lots of competition with big retailers for that business.

"The custom software development is running at just under a 40% margin and that's a fair bit lower than I expected. I price it for a 50% margin but apparently that's not happening. I think the problem there is that some of the projects are taking more time than I allow for in the quotes."

"Do you see anything positive going on?" Mark asked.

"Yeah, our proprietary software is running above breakeven now and it looks like it's almost ready to start to paying back the initial investment I made in it. With any luck we'll sell another ten licenses next year. A week ago I thought it was our problem but now I think it's a bright spot for us."

"Just out of curiosity, how receptive is the market to your proprietary software?" Dave asked.

"What do you mean?" I asked him.

"Well, are there lots of prospects? Is it an easy sale to make? When they look at it, do they like it? That's the type of stuff I'd like to know," Mark replied.

"Well, there are a limited number of companies that can use it. It's a fairly lengthy sales cycle and we have a few competitors now. All in all, the market's not as big as I thought it would be. In the beginning I thought we could build the company around it but now I know Velocity has to have the other profit centers," I said. "I think that the business model needs them, even if they are giving me some grief right now."

"All in all it doesn't sound too bad," said Mark. "Your current business model appears to be workable. It's not the same one you originally started out with. You started in one market and now you are in three, but that's not all that unusual. Like you said, the issue is that the profit centers aren't performing up to the standards that you need them to. I'm pretty sure it can be worked out. The idea now is to know what to keep on the radar and work on. That's what the forecast and variance report does for you. It raises flags on the parts of the business model that need attention. I agree that you should look into the field techs first. I'm certain that you can make some improvements there. We'll drill into the other profit centers after that."

We continued to talk as we worked. He used the rest of the time to introduce me to the AR^{2}T of momentum. We dialed in on the field techs, particularly on the third step: realizing the available options to improve the margins. Part way through, we called in the relief helpers and took a break. Teru came over and joined us, he brought me a pen and paper to write on. I wrote our ideas down and Mark informed me that this was just the first pass. There'd be more passes in the coming weeks and we'd involve the field techs in them as well. This AR^{2}T form was going to stay open until we had it nailed down.

I was surprised how much stamina Mark had for a man of his age. He worked steadily for four hours until the walls were completely full of cement. Then the beer was brought out.

We all found a place to sit. Teru took the time to thank everyone. There was a lot of good natured conversation. As I took the last sip of my beer Mark asked me a question.

"Dave, I've got an idea. There's a team practice at noon tomorrow. We've got a lot of drills planned. Phil and I could use an extra set of hands. Do you feel like helping out?"

"I'd like that. It will be fun to be out on the field with Ann again," I replied.

PART FIVE

As Told By Jen

23

Dave said, "Time is really rolling along, isn't it, Jen?" I agreed.

The break caught me by surprise. Time often flew by when I was listening to Dave talk about the old days with Mark. I was learning to take a lot of notes and save my questions for later.

It seemed like a good time to review.

"Dave can I ask you a few questions?" He nodded. "So far in the story Mark has introduced you to three of the five elements: the AR²T of momentum, the company promise, and financial information systems."

"That's right."

"Which one is the most important?"

"They're all important. In fact they all work together. If any one of the elements is missing or weak it impacts the whole company. Any weakness holds the company back from developing up to its full potential.

"However," Dave said as he leaned back and rubbed his chin, "Mark always referred to the company promise as the keystone element. I tend to agree with him. When the promise is dialed in on a good business opportunity and the company is committed to delivering on it, then you've got the central piece in place. Think about it in the reverse: if the company promise either doesn't connect with the market or the company doesn't consistently deliver on it then it will be very difficult to grow any kind of business at all.

"When I came up with the company promise for Velocity Software, 'we develop technology that helps smaller companies compete and win', it made a huge difference. It's still the same today except that our definition of small has gotten bigger. We review the company promise every year at our strategic planning meeting to make sure it still fits, but we've always kept it the same even as we expanded into new industry sectors, in fact it's led us in that direction. We look at markets that small businesses operate in and ask ourselves if there's a way to get in there and deliver on our company promise. Our curiosity has found us a lot of good business over the years."

"So once you get one you stick with it?" I asked.

"Absolutely, if it's a good one, but if it's not connecting you with a market that's willing to pay then you really need to re-think it and come up with something that works. Otherwise the company will struggle for who knows how long."

"I think I get it now," I replied.

"Jen, just to make sure, let me ask you a question. Who owns the business?"

"That's a trick question. Nobody owns a business; people own companies," I replied.

Dave had a big grin on his face. "That's partly right, but to find the answer to my question you have to go back to the first thing we discussed: **a company does business in a market**. If the people in the market like your company promise they'll give you their business and if your company doesn't keep its promise then they can take their business away. If they can give it and they can take it away then it appears to me that they own it."

I looked away for a moment and then turned back and smiled. "You didn't tell me that before, but it's pretty obvious now," I replied.

"I know, sorry about that. I just wanted to make sure the point was made. A strong company promise resonates well with the target market. If you don't have a strong company promise you should adjust it until you get it right. It's the keystone element because it has more business potential than any of the other elements, but at the same time all of the elements are important."

"Don't worry," I said. "I've got it now and I think I'm getting a handle on how the AR²T of momentum creates the right kind of momentum. Now I'm interested to hear more about how Mark helped you with Velocity's financial information system. Is there anything you want to add?"

"Sure. Financial information systems are the numbers part of the business game and they're just as important to building a strong company as throwing is to a softball team. Mark was fond of telling me that no matter what how old the players are or what their skill level is, they always throw the ball in their pre-game warm ups. It's the same when your company is doing business: you should always know your numbers. Your financial information system has to give you the numbers that clearly show how well your business model is performing and how money is flowing through your company.

"In the story I told you about how Mark started with a forecast and variance report and there is more to a strong financial information system than that. Carol really had the hardest part of that one. I don't think I fully understood the chart of accounts until sometime later. It was a real change of mindset for her.

She had to start thinking about what I needed to know and then she had to help design the systems that delivered useful information."

"Why was it up to Carol?" I asked.

"It wasn't entirely up to her. Mark gave her direction and advice, but most of the paperwork is handled by the bookkeeper. They see all of the source documents and they enter the data into the accounting program. What bookkeeping is supposed to do is process data into information so it's natural to make the bookkeeper responsible for the financial information system.

"An interesting fact about the reports from accounting programs is that they're all historical. If those are the only numbers that you look at when you're managing your company, then it's a bit like trying to drive while you're looking in the rear-view mirror. On the other hand, forecasts look out the windshield towards the future. Then as time passes your forecast is compared to the actual numbers from your accounting system. The variances give you some really useful feedback. It's a great way of testing the assumptions that went into your business model."

"How did that help you?"

"Well, like most people I made quite a few assumptions as I grew the business and I was finding out that they were wrong. Before the forecast and variance reports I couldn't figure out where I was going wrong."

"Can you give me an example?"

"Sure, let's go back to the field techs. I set our rates for the field techs at $75.00 per hour and I was paying them $22.00 per hour, so I assumed that I'd be making money hand over fist, but when Mark looked at the financials he pointed out that I was only charging $47.62 per hour."

"How did that happen?"

"Well, I was paying my techs for eight hours per day and wasn't selling all eight. What Mark did was take the total field tech revenues and divide them by the number of hours that I paid my techs for. He called it my effective charge out rate and he was right, that's all we were effectively charging for each hour that I paid for. All eight hours weren't sold every day. There was travel time, meetings, and admin functions. They're all part of the job and the company should cover the employees' time for that. What I discovered is that we weren't selling as many hours as I thought we were.

"The real difficulty comes when you assume that you're making good profits—but you're not."

"It still looks like you were making good profits" I said. "If you were charging $47.62 and paying $22.00 you were making $25.62 per hour."

"There are also other direct costs to consider like vehicle expenses, holiday pay, and employee benefits. They chew into it a bit and that's just the first base expenses. Getting to second base involves counting the overhead expenses that came along with offering the service like the square foot cost for their desk space, Carol's time to handle their incoming calls and do the invoicing for their clients, the sales and marketing expenses to land the clients, business cards, and cell phones. When you look towards third base there's even my time as their manager."

"Wow."

"A bit later Carol and I took a good hard look at it. We discovered that ever since day one we hadn't made it to third base on this profit centre. It'd taken up a lot of my time and energy but it hadn't added anything to the company's profits."

"Really?"

"To make matters worse I had to finance it. The employees were paid every two weeks with a one week hold-back, so the expenses had to be paid within fourteen days on average and the clients took an average of forty-six days to pay their invoices. That meant I was basically financing a non-profit division for thirty two days worth of business and I couldn't really afford that."

He paused for a few moments before he continued. "Like you, I assumed that our field techs were making good money and then when the company wasn't profitable—I couldn't understand why. It was frustrating. My financial information systems just weren't set up to give me the information that I needed to manage the company effectively."

"Stan was talking to Martin at Hydro and Grant at West Valley about key performance indicators. Are they part of financial information systems too?"

"They certainly are. Forecasts look into the future and the statements from the accounting program look back into recent history. A company owner should get them within twenty days after the month is over. KPIs are designed to be closer to real time. If I remember correctly Grant was using productivity and efficiency. Productivity is very close to the effective charge out rate. Both measure how well the employees' time is selling. Efficiency measures how effectively employees use the time that has been sold. In fact, that'd be a good KPI for Martin to start using at Hydro. It sounds like some of his jobs are taking more time to complete than he allows for in his quotes."

"Are there other KPIs?" I asked.

"Sure, there are hundreds of possible choices, like the number of quotes or proposals done per week, conversion rate of quotes into sales, average dollar sale, total daily sales, number of brand new customers, and in some case it could even be traffic in the showroom.

"Sometimes you'll hear people refer to a set of KPIs as a dashboard. At any rate, they should measure the factors that drive the success of the company. There's an old saying: 'you get what you measure'. I've found it to be true a lot more often than not. If you measure the right things and share the results with your team then they'll generally try to improve them. It's certainly a lot better than having your company's success drivers flying below everyone's radar."

"That makes perfect sense, but it's getting to be a lot to take in," I said.

"There's more to financial information systems than that. We haven't even talked about the balance sheet or statement of cash flows yet, but I'm not going to bore you with those right now. It occurs to me that when you're looking at a large, complex project like building a strong company, the simplicity you're after has a fairly high level of complexity of its own—it does take a bit to learn and absorb it."

"You're not kidding about that!"

"Okay Jen, do you want to get back to the story?"

"Sure," I replied.

PART SIX

As Told by Dave

24

When I told Ann that Mark had asked me to help out at practice her eyes lit up.

"That's awesome, Dad. It'll be fun just like in the old days when you used to coach my teams."

"Well maybe not quite," I said with a chuckle. It felt really good to see her so excited about spending time with me. Lately I'd been thinking that I didn't know her as well as I used to. The company had been pulling me away from the family and even when I was with them my mind was somewhat preoccupied most of the time. I'd almost forgotten what it was like to connect with her. She was growing up fast and I'd been missing out on it—even when I was there.

It took us a while to find my glove. It was in the back corner of the garage behind my golf clubs. They hadn't been used in a while either. Ann went upstairs to tell Karen that we found it.

"We found it, we found it!" I heard her call out as she ran off.

I stayed behind and looked around. There hadn't been any space to get my car inside the garage for over a year. I shook my head because I'd been frustrated by that, but it didn't matter anymore. Now it seemed like the best times of our lives were stored in our garage. I was starting to see things differently. There was my workbench and tools over by the window. It was a mess. I remembered that I used to like having time to work on projects around the house and in our backyard. On the other wall were the shelves where I could see our camping stuff, we'd taken some good trips. The Christmas and Halloween stuff was packed up on the top shelf. A lot of good memories came flooding back. I stayed in there for a while cleaning up the workbench and reminiscing by myself.

At 11:30 Ann opened the door and yelled, "It's time to go Dad, we don't want to be late."

It was only a fifteen minute drive to the ballpark so we arrived early. As we turned into the driveway the batting cage site was over to our right just beyond the tennis courts. All was quiet now, there was nobody there. The cement needed time to set. I felt a sense of pride as I looked at the forms rising up from the ground. It'd been a hard day's work yesterday, I still felt a bit sore but I didn't mind.

Ann was talkative on the drive up and I liked connecting with her again. She kept her world simple and somehow found a way to enjoy almost everything in her life.

Mark's truck was in the parking lot. He was already down at the field putting the bases out.

Ann got her equipment out of the trunk and we headed towards the dugout.

"Hi Ann, how are you doing?" Mark called out.

"Fantastic! It's a great day for ball," she hollered back.

As we got closer to the field I asked Mark, "What do you need me to do?"

"I haven't raked the infield yet, you can do that if you'd like. The rake is in the lockbox over by third and it's open now."

I went over and got the rake out and started to work around the infield. Ann's teammates were arriving steadily. Mark had a warm greeting for each and every one of them. He even had a few questions about schoolwork and other activities that were going on in their lives. They were all happy to see him. There were high fives all around. Pretty soon the dugout was full and alive with chatter. Mark and Phil were standing next to it laughing and joking with the kids.

"Alright ladies, it's twelve o'clock," Phil called out. The team filed out and formed a half circle in front of them. A few minutes later they cheered and started off jogging. Without any prompting they fell into formation running side by side, looking every bit the team in their blue and white practice jerseys. The chatter didn't slow down any as they ran around the field.

"Dave, come on over. We'll bring you up to speed on the practice plan for today."

I put the rake back into the lockbox and walked over to them.

"First they're going to finish their run. Then they'll go through their warm up stretches. Next it's the throwing and catching drills. That'll take them about twenty five minutes. Then I'll send three players over to you in left field. You'll be running a batting drill with the wiffle balls. One girl hitting at a time and the other two will be shagging the balls back to you. Phil will be doing fly ball drills over in left field with four players and I'll be working with the other five on grounders in the infield. Each of the players will rotate through all of the stations. That should take us to a bit after one o'clock and we'll take a water break then."

"Sounds good to me," I replied.

"Okay Phil, make sure they stay focused through their stretches. I'll help Dave get set up in right field," Mark said.

As we walked over to the dugout to get the wiffle balls, bats, and plastic home plate, Mark gave me the lowdown on how he wanted the wiffle ball drill to go.

"What we need them to focus on now is their timing. We already talked to them about it in the meeting. As you pitch talk to them about load and trigger. When you start into your windup they should be loading which is shifting their weight onto their back foot. The trigger is when they take a small step with their left foot and start moving their weight forward. When their trigger is timed right they'll be able to get the bat out front to meet the ball."

"Is there anything else that you'd like me to go over with them?" I asked.

"It's better to keep things simple at this point. Just make sure they are positioned right in relation to the plate and keep going over the load and trigger. Pitch to them with the full windmill motion so they get used to timing their trigger with the pitcher's motion."

After we set up the plate and dropped the bats next to it he paced off a few steps and poured the wiffle balls out onto the grass. "Pitch from here," he said. "These wiffle balls are kind of neat. They slow down a lot quicker than a softball so you have to be closer to the plate to get the same batters' reaction time as in a real game."

"Pitch thirty balls per batter and then you can send the batter over to Phil and he'll send a player into me and I'll send you another one from the infield. We'll move them all through each station."

"Okay, I can handle that."

The next thirty five minutes went by quickly. It took a bit of concentration to get the pitches into the strike zone. After I got into a rhythm I alternated between talking to the players and listening to Mark and Phil giving feedback on their drills. I remember being impressed by how positive they were even when they looking for corrections.

We all sounded like broken records and the kids didn't seem to mind. It occurred to me that it what we were working on was pretty clear to anyone within earshot. It wasn't supposed to be a secret or anything like that but the messages were obvious and I thought that I could see the kids improving right in front of my eyes.

After the last player was through it was time for the water break. Ann came running by with a big smile on her face. "This is great, isn't it, Dad? Are you having fun too?" she asked.

"You know what? I forgot how much I missed it. It is a lot of fun," I responded as she passed me heading to the dugout to get her water.

"Hey Dave, good job out there with the batters," Mark said. "It looked like their timing was really coming around."

"Thanks, the only problem is that I think I'll be saying 'load and trigger, that's it, good job,' in my sleep tonight," I laughed.

"Repetition is what it boils down to," Mark said. "We can't just show them how to do it once at the start of the season and expect them to do things perfectly for the rest of the season.

There's a business lesson in that for you."

I started to think of what to say next and before I could respond Mark turned to the dugout and said, "Okay ladies, circle up." They all came bounding out of the dugout onto the field and formed a half circle around him.

"I liked what I saw in the first set of drills. I could see that you all were concentrating and thinking about what you were supposed to be learning. Tell me, why is that important again?"

"Because practicing without thinking is just going through the motions!" they all shouted together.

"What are we here for?"

"To learn, improve, build a better team, and have FUN," they shouted again.

"Okay, for the next set of drills we'll need both our catchers in their gear. We'll get the pitchers going in left field with one catcher. The other catcher can join Phil in the infield for bunt defense drills with the rest of the team."

They all headed off and Mark came over to me. "I'd like you to catch for our second pitcher. Is that alright with you?" he asked.

"I suppose it is, although I haven't caught for a while."

Phil was assigning positions to the players and getting ready to pitch to the bunters. He was reviewing the team's strategy and even getting some players to put their helmets on and run the bases. He asked the batter to demonstrate the proper bunting technique before he threw the first pitch. As I headed out to left field I could hear him call out, "Does everybody know what they need to do?" The players all yelled, "Yeah." He followed that by saying, "Okay, let's get started."

When we got going with the pitchers Mark worked them through a series of drills. He seemed to have names for them all: the K, the step baby step, the twice around, the walk through, the stork, and hit the spot. I was glad that Mark brought out a bucket for me to turn upside down and sit on. It was a lot of work. I really had to pay attention. Those girls could really whip that ball with their windmill-style pitching.

As the drills were taking place Mark stood next to the pitchers. He gave them direction and feedback. At other times he asked questions. What are you thinking about? What do you think you need to be concentrating on? How did your hand feel on that one?

Off in the distance Phil sounded about the same. He had runners starting on different bases with the batters putting bunts down. Everyone had to concentrate as the drill simulated lots of real game situations. When they made defensive mistakes he stopped the drill and went over the correct positioning and assignments. He did it in such a positive way that nobody seemed to mind. In fact they seemed to enjoy it. There was lots of laughing involved.

The next half hour passed very quickly. When the practice ended Mark and Phil called the team together and reviewed the things that were worked on. They congratulated the kids on their concentration and pointed out the progress that they were making as a team. The goal was to become a good enough team to finish in the top two at district tournament and that would qualify them for the regional championships. Once they reached that goal they would set another.

After practice Mark asked if I could meet him at the Diamond Café at 2:30. I took Ann home and headed up. Ann was talkative again on the way home. She was telling me the proper way to field a ground ball and get the throw off quickly. She also talked about how the bunt defense changes when the runners are on different bases. She was learning a lot on the West Valley Rep Team and was excited about it.

She went on to talk about the contribution that Mark and Phil wanted her to make to the team and how she was accountable to the other players and responsible for her own position. She was excited that they wanted her to play first base and get really good at catching the throws that were off target. "If I can do that, then our whole infield will play with more confidence," she said.

After I dropped Ann off at the house I had a few minutes to myself on the drive up to the Diamond Café. I remember thinking about how great it would be if everyone at Velocity Software wanted to be accountable and contribute towards building our company as badly as the kids wanted to contribute to building their team.

Mark was already at the Diamond Café by the time I got there. I opened the door and looked around the café. He was at a table over in right field with Phil. A couple of Ann's team mates were sitting on the infield stools having milkshakes with their parents. I smiled and waved hello as I walked past them.

When I got closer to the table Phil called out, "Hey Dave! Long time, no see."

I laughed and replied, "I was just thinking that too."

Julie must have been expecting me. There was a cup of coffee already at the table. After I sat down Mark got right to the point. "I asked you here so we could go over how the West Valley Rep Team operates."

"Okay," I said.

"I not sure if you noticed, but there are five elements that we work on at every practice: throwing, catching, fielding, batting, and base running. Our main goal is to have each player improve at all the elements as the season goes on. That will make the team more competitive as we gear up for the playoffs and not to mention the players find it rewarding to improve."

I took a moment and thought back the practice for a bit before responding. "I can see it now. It was a good practice. We also worked on our pitching and the bunt defense."

Phil jumped in to the conversation. "In Mark's world those are just advanced levels of the elements. Pitching is throwing and the bunt defense is specialized fielding."

"He's right," Mark replied, "but that's not really why I called this meeting. Phil and I have been talking and we'd like you to join the team. How would you like to be our batting coach?"

"I'd like that, but I'm not sure I'm ready for it. It's a lot of responsibility. Don't you know somebody who could do a better job?"

The both laughed. "It's funny that you should use the word responsibility. We were just discussing your response-ability."

"What's that?"

"Well, here's an example. When a grounder gets hit towards the shortstop the player has to field the ball and make the throw to first base. If they can do that consistently they are response-able. They effectively respond to that type of situation when it arises."

"Okay, I get it. That's interesting, but how is it relevant?" I asked.

"Well, we're offering you the coaching position even though we're aware that you're not fully response-able yet. That means a few things. First, as the head coach I'll still be accountable. Second, that makes it my job to train you to be response-able. Third, there will have to be a lot of communication between all three of us before and after the practices and games. Phil and I think we can make it work."

"Well, if you're comfortable with it then I wouldn't mind giving it a try. I can't really say no anyways, isn't this part of the trade we're making? I help out with West Valley Softball and you help me out with Velocity."

Phil laughed out loud. "Another victim gets snared in the trap! I love it."

Mark jumped back into the conversation. "Listen here, you guys aren't victims. I'm doing right by both of you. On top of that it's easy to see how much the pair of you enjoy coaching."

We all laughed, Phil reached over and shook my hand. "Welcome aboard Dave, I'm looking forward to working with you."

PART SEVEN

As Told by Jen

25

Dave looked around his office, stood up, and moved his head side to side stretching his neck. "Jen, that's how I got hooked into coaching softball again. At the time I didn't realize that it was a lifetime contract." He smiled and shook his head. "Mark was a crafty guy."

"Dave, that's a great story," I replied.

"Let's head down to the coffee room again. I can always get more comfortable in there."

This time I took all my things with me. When we got to the coffee room I found a comfortable chair. The first thing Dave did was pour us both a glass of water. Then he got two chairs sat on one and swung his feet up on the other and started talking again.

"Mark and I stayed in the Diamond for at least another hour after that while he showed me the accountability matrix."

"Can you tell me more about the accountability matrix?" I asked.

"It's the fourth of his key elements. It's another example of simplicity on the other side of complexity. It appears complex when you first see it, but after you learn it, understand it, and absorb it you realize it's the simplest way to organize any team or company. You have to navigate through some complexity to get to the kind of simplicity that's really valuable. I suspect that's why Holmes said he would give his life for it. I can give you an overview today, but we don't have enough time to get into all the details."

Dave asked me for a pen and some paper.

"Mark called it a team accountability matrix in softball and a company accountability matrix, or CA³M, when he used it in the business world. They're both exactly the same only with different applications. He said that he got the idea from a project management tool and then he adapted it to make it work for going concerns."

He started drawing horizontal and vertical lines on the paper. "What the CA³M does is list all of the functions that the organization needs to perform down the first column. Then all of the people involved are listed across the top row.

Among other things it's used to assign the accountabilities and responsibilities to the people involved. It also identifies who needs to be communicating with whom and when. Everything that happens in the organization is right there in one place.

"Nowadays we build them on Excel spreadsheets and they can get to be pretty big, but it'll be easier for you to understand if I just draw a few pieces at a time."

Then he stopped and looked directly at me. "You know what's funny? Almost every company owner you talk to wants their people to be more accountable and responsible and to have them communicate better."

"That's true," I said. "But why is it funny?"

"How many of them have a plan to make that happen?"

"Not many, I suppose. There's nothing I've heard of anyways."

"That's generally been my observation too," Dave said. "Mark believed that it was important to deal with accountability head on, he also added responsibilities and communication. Over the years he also figured out how to turn the CA³M into a roadmap for the systemization of companies. It even evaluates the strength of the organization and tracks the job descriptions and performance plans. It's become a true matrix. The CA³M is the most complex of his five key elements."

"It sounds like it," I said.

"Well let me rephrase that: it is and it isn't," Dave replied. "Once they're built they seem fairly simple. Part of the challenge is that most owners haven't seen anything like it before. Once they understand it they'll be able to appreciate how simple it makes the challenge of building accountability into their organizations. The owner's role becomes a whole lot easier."

"Okay, I'm game, but can I ask another question?"

"Sure, what is it?"

"What does the small three above the A stand for?"

"Good question. It identifies what's involved in accountability. When somebody is accountable they are answerable for the results, they have the authority to make choices and decisions, and they're obligated to pay attention."

"How is that different from responsible?"

"There's a big difference. Take the shortstop example from earlier. The player is responsible for making the play, but Phil is accountable for ensuring the player is response-able. If the team's fielding is below standards then Phil is answerable, he also has the authority to choose the training and he has to pay attention to how they are improving.

"The easiest way to tell the difference is when a person is called on to perform the task they are responsible and if they are charged with getting the results they are accountable. In companies the size your whitepaper is focused on you'll see some functions where the same person is both accountable and responsible, but it's still important to identify both."

"Okay, I think I've got it now."

"Here's a small CA³M," Dave said as he turned the paper in front of him and slid it towards me. "I've really condensed it."

FUNCTIONS	Current Strength	Documented	Frequency	Head Coach	Fielding Coach	Batting Coach	Team Parent
Number of People				1	1	1	1
Job Descriptions	B+	Yes	16	Yes	Yes	Yes	Yes
Performance Plans	B+	Yes	16	Yes	Yes	Yes	Yes
COACHING							
Practice Plans	A+	Yes	30	AR	C	C	I
Pregame Plans	A+	Yes	30	AR	C	C	I
Catching	B	Yes	720	I	AR		
Fielding	A –	Yes	720	I	AR		
Batting	B	Yes	720	AIC		R	
Throwing	B	Yes	720	AR			
Base running	A –	Yes	720	AR			

I looked at it for a minute. "Now I have a few questions. I understand that A is for accountability and R is for responsibility, but what do the I and the C mean?"

"They're the communications part. The I stands for inform, which means that the person with the I in their column needs to be informed of the happenings in the function. The C stands for consult, which means that the person needs to be consulted beforehand. The practice plans, here in the first column are a good example. When you look across, Mark was accountable and responsible. Phil and I needed to be consulted to make sure the drills we needed were included and finally the team parent was informed so she could let the players know when to show up and what to expect."

"Near the top of the CA³M there are rows for Number of People, Job Descriptions, and Performance Plans. Can you tell me more about those?" I asked.

"No problem. It isn't obvious in such a small sample, but often in a company or on a team you have a number of people doing the same job. The row for number of people just tells you how many people have that position. A restaurant might have eight servers for example.

"Below that is a row for job descriptions. This is used to indicate whether or not there is a current written job description prepared for each position. Every company should have job descriptions that clearly outline the expectations. They make everything flow better.

"Below that is the row for performance plans. Be careful not to confuse them with performance reviews. Performance plans look out the windshield, they clarify the desired future performance and identify the improvements required to make it happen. They also outline a plan to move forward with. Performance reviews look in the rear-view mirror. All too often they create tension between the manager and the employee."

"I'm following you Dave, but what are the 16s in the frequency column for?"

"Ahh, you picked up on that quickly. The Frequency column is used to indicate how many times a year the function is performed per year. I put in the sixteens because there are twelve players, three coaches, and one team parent in the example I just drew for you. Everyone gets a job description and a performance plan so both functions have a frequency of sixteen."

"That must mean Mark is going to prepare thirty practice plans."

"That's right and the 720 frequency for the elements comes from thirty practices plus thirty pregame warm-ups. That makes sixty. The sixty gets multiplied by all twelve players for the total frequency of 720. In this scenario the coaches we will be involved in 720 one on one coaching sessions for each of the five elements."

"This is starting to make sense. You've identified a coaching frequency and you have a performance plan, plus you've got a series of practice plans that are going to be developed in concert with the other coaches. I can see how that would produce good results."

"That's a good observation, you're catching on quickly. There's a fair amount to learn though. I remember having lots of 'Ah Ha' moments when I put my first few CA³Ms together. It's a remarkably effective approach to organizing everything that a team or company needs to do. I've told you about the main concepts, but there are still more pieces to the CA³M puzzle that I'll tell you about later."

"Can I ask you one last question before we move on?" I asked.

"All right, give me your best shot."

"What are the columns for Current Strength and Documented for?"

"Current Strength is used to rate how well the function is being performed. I like to use the same letter grade system that I learned in elementary school. Everybody seems to understand it.

"Documented is interesting. This is where it really becomes a matrix. When there's a system, policy, or procedure associated with the function it's noted here. I just put yes on the example I drew, but normally there's a locator there that tells you where to find it in the team or company manual. It might read CM-2.4 if it's in the company manual, chapter two, section four, for example."

"That's pretty neat."

"I'll tell you how it expands. Imagine the CA³M I drew with all the players are also added across the top row. Then going down the spreadsheet imagine the nine positions on the field as functions in the first column below the elements. Even imagine the elements expanding. Batting also includes reading signals, regular bunt, sacrifice bunt, slap bunt, push bunt, and slash bunt. All of the other elements will expand as well."

"Wow that will get to be pretty big in a hurry."

"Yeah, and it's all useful too. That afternoon in the Diamond Café Mark showed me the matrix and then as we left he handed me the batting system to read. He already had a performance plan in place for me and he was leading me through it. I was response-able in no time."

26

"There's a system for batting?" I asked incredulously.

"Sure, I'll get it for you. Wait here it's on the wall in my office."

Dave disappeared for a couple of minutes. I got up and refilled our water glasses. Just as I was sitting down again he showed up at the door carrying a framed picture.

"Here it is. I've kept it as a souvenir to remind me how straightforward it is to build systems," Dave said as placed the framed copy on the table in front of me. "It's the original one I got from Mark. Some people think I'm crazy for keeping it all of these years."

Title: Batting

Step 1: On Deck Circle
- Positive thoughts only—block the negative ones
- Swing while holding two bats—twice
- Time your practice swings with the pitcher's pitches
- Offer encouragement to our batter at the plate

Step 2: Getting Set in the Batter's Box
- Look to the third base coaches' box to get your signal
- Have a loose grip on bat—knuckles to knuckles
- Know what the pitch count is—if you don't, ask the umpire
- What type of pitch are you expecting?
- Take your position in the batter's box—solid stance—feet shoulder width apart
- Stand up tall and athletic with your head turned towards pitcher, chin tucked in

Step 3: Load

- Load by shifting your weight to your back foot raising the heel of your front foot
- Bend knees slightly
- Draw hands towards back shoulder so your top thumb can almost touch it
- Focus your eyes on the spot the pitcher will release the ball from

Step 4: Trigger

- Time your trigger with the pitcher's motion and expected speed of the pitch
- Take a small step towards the pitcher with front foot, turning your toes out
- Pivot on your back foot
- Open the hips to the pitcher
- Maintain your shoulders parallel to create spring in your core muscles

Step 5: Choose

- Move hands forward towards the ball—not down or out and away from your body
- Lead with the butt of the bat
- Determine if the pitch is a ball or strike
- Choose to swing and hit the ball
- Or stop and return the bat to your shoulder

Step 6: Swing the Bat

- Contact the ball out in front—before it reaches the plate
- As you rotate your shoulders extend your arms into the power V
- Accelerate the bat head with your wrists
- As you swing keep your right palm up facing to the sky (Right handed batters)
- Roll the bat only after you've hit the ball

Step 7: Follow Through

- Power through the ball
- The heel on the back foot should be up with just your toes on the ground

- Finish with good core rotation, belt buckle towards the pitcher
- Finish with hands behind you at shoulder height

"This is for hitting, but how does it relate to business?" I asked him.

"Well, that's what systems look like," he said with a laugh. "If you took a quick glance at it without reading any of the words it would look exactly like one of the twenty-eight systems we've got operating here at Velocity Software.

"The first thing that I should tell you is that having the system made it much easier for me to teach the players how to hit. I knew what to look for and it was easy to figure out what they should be working on. There is another system for coaching batters that recommends practice drills. Mark and Phil basically made it a plug and play system. They had them for all areas of the game. This is the core of the West Valley Rep system."

"So that's why they are so successful year after year," I commented.

"That's right, and the second big thing that I should tell you is that today's systems are improved versions of the one you're looking at. Particularly the coaching system has changed with the new video technology and training aids on the market. All of the West Valley systems get reviewed every year to see where they can be improved."

"That's remarkable," I said.

"The same process is one of the main reasons Velocity Software went on to become so successful. We use the CA^3M to coordinate the systemization of the company and to document our policies. Everyone here clearly knows what they are accountable for and responsible for. It's really helped us to build a rock solid company. It's even turned out to be one of our best competitive advantages. We're known for user friendly software because we write good manuals that include easy-to-follow systems. In fact, our system has us thinking about the manuals and end users on the front end right in the design phase. We make mock ups of the manuals and meet with the end users to get their input and feedback. It makes our designs better and the eventual implementations go much easier."

"I can see how that would happen," I said.

Dave continued. "Having a complete set of documented systems for a company or a team is one thing, but the thinking that goes into improving them and maintaining their use is what really brings the efficiency to life. It takes some commitment on the part of the owner but it's definitely well worth the effort."

"Isn't that like micromanaging?" I asked.

"It's the opposite. If you're people aren't following the system it's important to find out why. Your clients won't pay extra to support your inefficiency for too long and if you allow the inefficiency to continue then the company will be giving up its profits—perhaps even part of your wages too. I've been there and it's not a lot of fun. On the other hand if you look into it and your people have found a better way that's great. Improvements are called positive deviances and they should be incorporated into the company's systems."

"Now we're talking about deviance!" I couldn't help myself, I laughed out loud.

Dave looked at me and smiled. "Sure, it's a loaded word, but it fits. When something happens that produces better than expected results it's a deviation to the positive side. These are like gold because they raise flags and identify new areas for improvements that could become excellent competitive advantages. Sometimes it makes sense to change your systems. Every company has to continually improve to stay competitive. Competitiveness is right in our company promise so we have to take it seriously ourselves. We have to walk the walk."

"I get it," I remarked, "it just sounds funny."

"Let me tell you one of the ways we use it. When we have a client that is really great to work with and we see ourselves really living our company promise and delivering exceptional value, the next step is identify as many similar companies as we can. Then we write a case study, get testimonials from the end users and their managers, ask them for referrals and prospects, and then call the prospects to identify the purchasers within the companies. Then we send it over to our sales department to draft a cover letter and follow up. We also make sure that it goes up on our website. It's a positive deviation that we track down and replicate."

"That's pretty neat."

"It's also one of our marketing systems. Some prospects receive five, six, seven, or more case studies from us before they become clients. We get a lot of credibility because of this system. Prospects know that we can deliver. Everybody here buys into it because that's where a lot of our best work comes from."

"I can see how it would bring in clients, but how is it a system?" I asked.

"All right then," Dave said with a smile on his face, "are you up for a challenge?"

"Sure," I said, although I was thinking that it might not be a good idea.

"I'll get you one of our system templates. Based on what I've told you already we'll see if you can fill it in and create a documented system." He got up and said, "I'll be right back."

A couple of minutes later he reappeared at the door. "The best way to learn is by doing something yourself and I'm going to challenge you to write a system. Let's use the last example of the positive deviance and because I've put you on the spot I'll take all the questions you throw at me."

I looked at the two page template that he handed me. It had a place for a title, a standard, and it was followed by seven steps with bullet points underneath each one. Dave explained that systems don't have to have seven steps but being as close a possible makes them easier to understand and remember. He said our minds are basically seven-bit processors. Most people can remember lists of seven but make lists eight items or longer and most people start having difficulties.

As I got started I looked at my notes and asked Dave a few questions. About twenty-five minutes later, after a lot of questions and some pointers from Dave, this is what I came up with.

<u>Title:</u> **Ideal Clients**

<u>Standard:</u> **Excellent Direction for Velocity's Sales Dept**

Step 1: Identify the Exceptional Clients Velocity is Working With
- Develop relationships with end users and management
- At weekly programmers meeting bring forward clients for discussion
- Describe the clients' qualities and features
- As a team, rate the clients' results & recommend candidates for follow up
- Articulate the value being delivered

Step 2: Identify Prospects Who Have Similar Problems and/or Challenges
- Notify sales department
- Check Velocity's prospects database for similar prospects

- Check our database for past clients who could use this added value
- Search by industry—SIC code
- Search market segments—for non-competitors serving the same market
- Search by company size & geographic area for comparables
- Search by their equipment on shop floor—ask distributer sales reps

Step 3: Draft Case Study
- Ask for the client's permission
- Use our templates, review previous case studies for style & formatting
- Background about the client, the presenting challenge or problem
- Describe their journey. What did they try before connecting with us?
- Emphasize our company promise
- Describe the design, build phases of the software development
- Describe the implementation
- Describe the results and benefits

Step 4: Testimonials
- Always pay attention to positive comments and ask if you can use them
- Use Velocity's standard questionnaires to draw them out
- Engage the clients in conversations particularly when they're happy
- Follow up

Step 5: Referrals
- Ask end users if they know anyone else who could use the service
- Ask if there are any industry events they can bring you to
- Ask who their key suppliers are and if they would introduce you
- Always do little extras to exceed their expectations

Step 6: Website Updating
- When the project is finished complete the case study
- Bring forward to weekly programmers meeting for review
- Provide the webmaster the case study and testimonials
- Update website

Step 7: Contacting Prospects
- Identify the purchasing agent within the prospect companies.
- Draft a letter—see previous letters file
- Send the letters
- Follow up call to gauge interest
- Close to a meeting and or put on Velocity's mailing list

"That's good, it's actually pretty close to the system we use," Dave said. "If you look at it again you can see how it would continue to improve with ongoing use. When we first started working with it about twenty years ago there was some push-back from the staff. Over the years we've worked the bugs out and everyone's bought into it because they realize it helps set the direction for the type of projects we take on and the type of clients we deal with. New people into the company don't even question it. They see it as part of who we are and how we do things. We've built a great database and scores of case studies. Using the system has gotten us a lot of contacts and tons of credibility. It's driven a lot of good business our way. I'd have to say that it's one of our core systems."

"I can see how that would happen," I said, "but isn't that a lot to ask from your programmers?"

"One of the things I learned from Mark is if you want to play at a high level, you have to practice. To make it easier I've split up the work. There are at least four people involved in the system, sometimes more: the sales admin, the salesperson, the programmer, and the webmaster," Dave said. "We could have easily identified them on your draft of the system."

"Okay, that makes sense."

"That system is on the sales and marketing side of things. We also developed systems for just about everything else, including all of our production."

"Interesting," I said. "I've read lots of authors who highly recommend systemizing companies, but I haven't come across anything yet that actually describes how to do it. That was a good experience, thanks Dave."

144

"There are lots of benefits to developing systems. One of them isn't thought of often enough. Over the life of a successful company the clients ultimately pay for everything, the direct costs, overheads, your wages, and even the company's profits. They're more willing to support an efficient company. Systemization leads you in that direction."

"That goes back to the business model doesn't it?"

"That's right. Systems make for an efficient business model with lower first base direct costs and lower second base overhead costs. It makes it a lot easier to be competitive and consistently score runs."

"I can see that," I said.

27

We took a short break and refilled our glasses of water. It gave me a chance to think through everything Dave and I had been talking about. I was curious to know more.

"Did you learn anything else from coaching with Mark and Phil?" I asked him.

"Sure I did, but like a lot of things they're only obvious when you know what you're looking for," Dave replied with a grin.

"Tell me more," I prompted.

"First off, they had great relationships with the kids. They took the time to get to know them and what was going in their lives. At the same time there was no question as to who was in charge and what was expected of the players. It's difficult to find that balance especially for the owner of a small company. In softball when you step though the gate and onto the field you leave everything else behind and assume the role of coach. It needs to be the same way in your company. You need to assume the role of the company owner. It's challenging to effectively set and maintain standards while building good relationships with your staff, but it needs to be done. The company owner's mindset and actions around this makes a huge difference."

"I imagine it does."

"It's especially difficult at the stage of growth your whitepaper is focused on. A lot of owners want their companies to be like families, but that can backfire in a lot of different ways, far too many to discuss here. Mark and Phil had great relationships with the kids and all the players all got along very well. They created a great environment year after year and they taught me that it was a skill that anyone can develop.

"The second big lesson was that the turnaround was going to happen through a series of steps and each of them had to be reinforced until they became habits. Everything wasn't going to improve all at once. That's why Mark started me working with the batters on their timing using load and trigger as the key words. At the café he explained it was still early in the year and we were going to be facing some fast pitchers as the season unfolded, especially when the team got to the district and regional tournaments. By then it would be too late to try and teach them how to adjust to the speed of the pitches."

"That's interesting but how does it apply?"

"Well, I'll bet in all research you've done on management you haven't yet come across the single most important skill for a manager."

I laughed, "I won't know if I have or not, at least until you tell me what it is."

"It's building and maintaining good habits in yourself and others. That's what we were coaching the kids do at the practices—build their habits. When we built enough of the right ones they became very response-able even when the competition became more intense.

"I can tell you that my instincts were to give the kids some other advice about their swings but I stuck to the script because that's what I was asked to do. I learned that focusing on one thing at a time and sticking with it until it became second nature was the best way to make significant lasting progress. For one thing the kids can feel themselves improving and it also forced me to think about how to sequence their training. Expecting too many improvements at once makes the learning process too confusing for everyone involved.

"In my case the kids got their timing down and started making contact with the ball. Then they really started believing they could hit the pitching at this level. Confidence is important. When they got their bat on the ball during the games they made the connection between what they practiced and their on-field results. Then they believed they could continue to practice and improve. That's when we started to build some good momentum and I turned their attention to other parts of the batting system."

"Again how does that translate to the business world?" I asked.

"When you try to improve too many things at once, you won't get the results you want on any of them. It will feel like you're running in circles and chasing your tail. The idea is to make each step achievable and plan to build on it," Dave replied.

"Can you give me an example?"

"Okay, the first part of Velocity's turnaround was to get the tech's effective charge out rate up to $59.50. Mark clearly let me know that I was accountable. I talked to my field techs about billable hours. Then we introduced them to the AR²T of momentum and started an AR²T form. I set KPIs for the field techs and made sure they knew that it was their responsibility to meet them. We also made it their responsibility to hand in their time cards daily, instead of just before payday. Next we held an ongoing series of weekly meetings where we discussed and built the inventory of ideas in the realize the options box. We always finished by reviewing everyone's TRaction plans for the week. We maintained the focus and kept it on the radar until we achieved the results that we were looking for. It wasn't an easy transition to make. We worked at it, one piece at a time, for three months.

"At first the techs didn't believe that we could achieve it, but we got some early wins from scheduling better and charging travel time for emergency calls. We also started pre-booking appointments. That was our first version of managed services. We kept building on our wins. Another theme was getting the techs to believe our service was worth that much. That turned out to be more challenging than I thought it should have been. After that more and more good habits fell into place and we actually got the effective charge out rate up over $60.00."

"Just out of curiosity, do you remember what else was on the AR²T form?"

"That was interesting. Under assessment we wrote the truth, that we were just breaking even and the company was financing the business. I have to tell you that at first, just like you, the techs didn't believe me, but we produced the numbers and showed them. That really opened their eyes.

"Under the first R for realize the results we simply put an effective charge out rate of $59.50.

"I can't remember all of the ideas that we came up with to go under the second R of realize the available options. There was a series of steps that went into it. The more we discussed it at our weekly meetings and drilled into it—the more good ideas that surfaced," Dave paused. "I knew for sure that I needed to improve along with the techs. I needed to get better at giving feedback and reinforcing our company promise. That was the first habit I worked on for myself.

"You know, I'd been sending out field techs for years without paying much attention to them, except when they called in with problems they couldn't solve on their own. I learned that I should have been setting standards for the delivery of value to Velocity's clients and standards for the profitability of the company.

"I learned a lot from the softball practices. I could see that Mark and Phil were experts at giving feedback and I could see the kids improving because of it. It's all part of the managing step on the poster that we were talking about earlier.

"Before Mark we'd fallen into the habit of responding to breakdown calls when our clients' computers either crashed or started performing poorly. We really weren't being proactive and delivering consistently reliable systems and software. We weren't in tune with our company promise mostly because I hadn't defined it yet. When our clients called with problems we'd just drop everything to get them up and running again. Sometimes it involved two hours of travel there and back just to bill out one hour. Counting the gas we weren't even getting to first base on those calls. Everyone seemed to think that we were doing good work, but that wasn't the reality. We didn't have profit center reporting or KPIs in place to let me know that we weren't doing a good job.

"A couple of weeks into the process we started developing a system for field tech site visits which included checklists for each of our regular clients. The field techs needed to develop good habits around those. We also started recommending software and hardware upgrades that would help make the clients more competitive in their markets. We looked at the services we were already delivering them to see what was predictable and discussed how we could be proactive about it. We kept meeting weekly as a team to review the KPIs and discuss problems that came up. Our company promise was always at the top of the agenda. As the weekly meetings continued we got more good ideas and kept moving new items to the TRaction plan as the earlier ones were implemented."

"It sounds like it worked well."

"It sure did. I had the huge advantage of having Mark coaching me. He and I met before the weekly meetings and discussed the habits Velocity needed to develop to be successful. He also gave healthy helpings of encouragement. What I mean by that is he made sure we understood that when committed to making improvements we could actually achieve quality results. It's important to recognize and reward progress.

"Mark was big on the AR²T of momentum. He helped me see the realize the options box as an inventory of ideas to experiment with. We didn't always know what was going to work and what wasn't. We'd make our choices and put them into TRaction plans to test them out. Some worked and some didn't, others needed to be adjusted. Having an inventory also allowed us to think about effective sequencing as we moved ideas onto the TRaction plans. We kept working at it until we surpassed our initial target of an effective charge out rate of $59.50. We had that AR²T form open for three months."

"That's great'" I said.

"I had a front row seat to watch Mark and Phil coach softball and I learned that it's rewarding to focus on improvements. They had a pretty good idea about how strong the elements needed to be for the West Valley softball team to reach its goals. They worked steadily on them using the accountability matrix to guide them. Mark and Phil had coached teams to districts and regionals before. Every year they started with a new group of kids and built them into very competitive teams. Their track record was pretty good. Phil said that experience had taught him not to fall into the trap of wishing he had better players. He knew it was much more productive to concentrate on coaching the players they had on the team to improve."

"Does that translate over into companies?"

"When you think about it the same concept is at the core of building a successful company. Mark and I were also working on the five key elements to strengthen my company. Before that Velocity had done a lot of business without having a strong company. It didn't take long before the symptoms started to overwhelm me.

"Back at that point in time it would have been easy to reach the conclusion that I couldn't successfully run the company. That's what I was thinking that day I went to the bank. Mark took the approach that I had the right raw material and with some direction, training, and coaching I could lead the company to success. He also had me take that same approach with the people who worked at Velocity. It all turned out very well. All that being said though, attitude is important. They selected their players for the West Valley Rep Teams based on it and he taught me to hire employees with good attitudes."

"So you got all of that from coaching with them?" I asked.

"Well yeah, not right away though. Like I said before, it's obvious now, but it did take me a while to see it.

Wow Jen, I just noticed that it's getting late and we've covered quite a bit for one day. You probably need some time to get ready for your big presentation with Jones tomorrow. How about we call it a day?"

I agreed and packed my things. Dave walked me out to my car. On the way he told me that I was learning a lot. He figured that I was going to do a great job with my presentation. Then he headed back inside to get his jacket and lock up before going home himself.

PART EIGHT

As Told by Jen

28

I had plans to meet Alice at the coffee shop after her exam. She had been studying hard and wanted to kick back and relax after the test. I really admired her for taking the initiative to upgrade her skills to get a better job. She went straight into the workforce after high school and was unfortunately getting typecast as a receptionist. She'd been putting in a lot of extra hours to break out and develop a career for herself.

Alice was supposed to arrive at about 9:30. I headed over at 7:30 with the notes from my meetings with Dave and the clients. I also brought along a few well-researched books on building high performance and expertise. I'd read them a few months earlier and I was getting a gut feeling that there were some direct correlations between the research and the story Dave was telling me.

It felt like I was back in college again cramming for an exam. I couldn't help but think of it how it paralleled Alice's current experience.

As I pulled into the parking lot I could see Haley's beat up old Ford Taurus in the employees' stall. I suddenly realized how much I missed our easy going conversations.

I opened the door and almost immediately heard Haley's friendly voice. "Hey Jen, it's really good to see you again. How have you been?"

"Not bad at all. Thanks for connecting me with Dave. He's been a wealth of great information."

"I figured that he'd give you a hand," she replied with a smile.

"I've got a pile of notes from my meetings with him. I thought that I'd come here and find a quiet corner to sit in and go over them."

"No problem, do you want your regular?"

"Sure, thanks Haley."

"My break isn't for another hour. Are you still going to be around then?" she asked.

"Yeah, I was actually planning on staying for a while. I'm meeting a friend from the office here at about 9:30. On the bright side, I'll probably be able to use a break myself in about an hour. This project is a bit of challenge to wrap my mind around."

"I remember that it had something to do with a quote about complexity and simplicity and building a rock solid company. It does sound challenging," she commented as she handed me a cup of hot coffee.

I settled into a comfortable chair by the fireplace and I started thinking about the complexity quotation again. By now I'd figured out that building a strong company was indeed a complex challenge and to make it even more difficult, every owner seemed to be pursuing their own unique type of business. Not too long ago making all that simple in a whitepaper seemed almost impossible, but now it looked like there was a solution on the horizon.

I picked up my stack of meeting notes and started reading through them.

After a while I switched to the notes that I'd made a couple months before when I was doing some reading on the development of high performance and expertise.

Karl Anders Ericsson is a key player in this area. He is world renowned and considered to be the leading expert on experts. He's done a lot of research himself on how expertise is developed and he's also extensively studied the other leading researchers in the field.

My attention was drawn to a section of a paper he wrote back in 1992 that I'd highlighted. At the time I figured that it was important but now it really started to resonate with me. The hairs on my arms seemed to stand up as I read it and then reread it again.

> Here's a typical example: Medical diagnosticians see a patient once or twice, make an assessment in an effort to solve a particularly difficult case, and then they move on. They may never see him or her again. I recently interviewed a highly successful diagnostician who works very differently. He spends a lot of his own time checking up on his patients, taking extensive notes on what he's thinking at the time of diagnosis, and checking back to see how accurate he is. This extra step he created gives him a significant advantage compared with his peers. It lets him better understand how and when he's improving. In general, elite performers utilize some technique that typically isn't well known or widely practiced.

It seemed to me that this is exactly what Dave was trying to explain while he was telling me about softball with Mark and Phil. They consistently gave their teams a significant advantage by working on the five elements, using systems, developing habits and setting standards. Also by giving their players good feedback on how they were improving. Plus they were always thinking about better coaching techniques and how to improve their own systems. It seemed to be a lot like the highly successful diagnostician that Ericsson wrote about.

I leaned back in the chair and took a sip of coffee it was cold by then, but I didn't really care.

Then it hit me.

The whitepaper should be about delivering significant advantages to owners who want to design and build strong companies.

Wow, like the concept of '**a company does business in a market'**. Not to mention the Five Key Elements of Company Strength: The AR²T of Momentum, Company Promise, Financial Information Systems, Company Accountability Matrix, and Marketing Plans, which I needed to learn more about soon. The whitepaper should describe them well enough that company owners understand how powerful they are and it should also teach them how to implement them in their own companies.

"Hey Jen, are you still drinking that coffee?" Haley asked as she walked over to the table.

"Yeah, but it's a bit cold now. I've been deep in thought. I'm prepping for a big meeting with Mr. Jones tomorrow. You know what? I think I'm starting to get a handle on this project now."

"You have a big meeting?" she asked.

"Oh yeah that's right, I haven't been around for a while, so I haven't told you yet."

I spent the next few minutes telling Haley about how Alice told me about the grumblings in the office and how I went on to get myself in over my head and how Stan helped me get through it.

"Gee, I haven't seen you this happy in a while and you sure get a sparkle in your eyes when you talk about Stan. You've got to spill the beans here. Tell me more about him."

I could feel myself getting embarrassed again. "There is nothing going on there," I replied.

"Keep telling yourself that," Haley said with a sly smile.

We kept on chatting for a few minutes. Alice arrived early looking very happy.

"The exam wasn't as challenging as I thought that it was going to be! I buzzed right through it. I knew the answers to all of the questions and the assignments weren't difficult at all," she said excitedly as she approached the table.

"Congratulations, that's great!" Haley replied.

"I knew that you were going to do well, you've been studying hard," I said.

Alice said, "It feels really good," as she put her books down, pumped her fist, and headed over to the counter to order a cup of coffee.

The three of us sat and chatted for a few more minutes until Haley had to get back to work.

After she left Alice asked, "So that's a fairly big pile of books and notes that you've got there. What's it all about? Is it part of your project?"

I explained to her the realization that I'd come to earlier. "The five key elements are all about delivering significant advantages that help people navigate through the complex project of designing and building a strong company."

I described the distinctions around, **a company does business in a market** and went over the Five Key Elements.

Haley was particularly interested in the forecast and variance reports. "In class they mentioned forecasting but we didn't really go into it at all. You're exactly right when you say that bookkeeping is all historical. It's all behind you. I like your analogy of looking out the windshield instead of trying to drive while you're looking in the rear-view mirror. There has to be some advantages to that."

"Yeah," I replied. "Then the variance reports show how well the business model is working. It compares the forecast to the actual numbers and lets everyone know what's going right and what needs some work. It's identical to the strategy the highly successful medical diagnostician in Ericsson's study was using. This type of systematic approach is at the very core of high performance."

As Alice kept talking I could tell that she was excited about the concept and understood that a forecast should be put together starting with the current run rates. She also agreed that a good chart of accounts would allow a company's profit and cost centers to be clearly identified.

"Alice, I've got a couple of clients working on setting up their first ones right now."

"Who are they?" she asked.

"It's Martin at Hydro Plumbing and Grant from West Valley Auto."

"I know them, they're regular CJN clients. We do their year-end reports and tax preparation for them. They're both pretty friendly."

"I've got an idea," I said. "I really don't know all that much about accounting. How would you like to help them with it?"

"I don't know," she replied. "I haven't done one before and I'm not exactly sure how to go about it."

It took some convincing and a quick call to Stan to see if he would help her out with it but Alice eventually agreed. Then she started to get excited about putting her newly learned skills to use. We talked for a while longer and made plans to call Martin and Grant in the morning to ask them if it was okay. If they agreed we'd ask them to send Alice their last twelve monthly statements and she'd pull their last two year ends from the CJN files. That would give her a good start. With Stan's help we might have the first drafts of their forecasts ready in time for my meeting with Mr. Jones.

29

Today was the big day. At 3:30 PM I was scheduled to meet with Mr. Jones and give him an update on the project. I had a fitful sleep. I'd woken up several times thinking about my presentation. I wanted it to be excellent.

I chose to go by the coffee shop before heading in. I didn't feel like going to the staff coffee room at CJN anymore. Ever since I found out that the folks at Carey Jones Norton were talking behind my back I saw them a little differently. Making small talk with them seemed uncomfortable now.

I arrived at the office before eight. Alice wasn't at the reception desk yet. I headed straight to my office and fired up the computer.

The first thing I did was take out my notes from that first meeting with Mr. Jones and go over them one more time. It was to be a whitepaper that helps people build and grow a successful business. I chuckled at that. My presentation was going to be about building a strong company. The content needed to be rock solid in keeping with the reputation of the firm. It also had to be something that owners could start implementing right away and finally it had to consider the Oliver Wendell Holmes complexity quotation.

I would not give a fig for simplicity this side of complexity,
but I would give my life for simplicity on the other side of complexity.

Now that I'd reviewed the parameters of the project, I got out another piece of paper and wrote down the main headings. Below them I started making notes about what was going to be included.

Alice popped her head into my office. "Good morning! I just got in touch with Grant and Martin. I told them that I was working with you on the forecast and variance reports and they were kind of happy that I'm helping out. They weren't quite sure how to start. Anyways, they're both sending over their last twelve monthly statements and they don't have a problem with us looking at their last two year-ends. We're off to the races."

"That's great news. Thanks very much."

"And Jen, that's not the best part. I also spoke with Stan and he's coming over at noon with sandwiches to help you prepare for your presentation with Mr. Jones. I've booked Conference Room #1. You're all set to go."

"Alice, you're a saint. I don't know how I can ever thank you."

"No worries. Stan wanted me to ask you to call him as soon as you got in but you must have snuck by me somehow. You should give him a call straight away."

"Thanks again, I'll get right on it."

I picked up the phone and dialled. "Hey Stan, how's it going?"

"Not bad," he replied. "You sure keep me busy though. It's a good thing Dave is on board with this or I'd be catching some flack around here."

"Sorry about that. I sure appreciate it though. I have to tell you that I wasn't expecting you to come over here today."

"I wanted to talk with you first and make sure that you don't mind me poking my nose into your business. As long as you don't think that I'm overstepping my boundaries I'm happy to help. I figure you might want to run through your presentation before you give it to good old Mr. Jones."

"You know what? That's a great idea, I'm kind of nervous about it and this will help me to collect my thoughts before I head into his office."

"Okay, it's a date then. Can I ask where you're at with the preparation?"

"Well, I've got the parameters for the project written down and I've started listing the content that I'm thinking about including in the presentation. It feels like I'm making some headway but then it all starts swimming around in my head again. I can't seem to get it all to crystallize in my mind."

"Hmm, it sounds like you're way out in the field of complexity again. Okay, let's narrow it down a bit. What is it that you want this meeting to accomplish?"

"I'd like to still have my job at the end of the day," I said a bit tersely.

Stan laughed. "I get that and I'd like to know what you think should be in the presentation to get that result."

"Stan, shut up."

"Whaaat?" he said slowly.

"I know what you are doing and I've got it right here in front of me. You're working the AR^{2}T of momentum but I've got to show him more than that."

It felt good to be able to banter with him. I was getting more comfortable with him. Now we could give each other friendly jabs without worrying about how the other would take it. I could almost see him smiling on the other end of the line.

"My point is, until you know the results you want, you won't be able to figure out what should or shouldn't be in the presentation. On a short time-frame like this you've got to boil it down to something that's manageable."

"Okay, here it is. I want him to know that even though I got off to a slow start I'm making some good progress now. I'm getting a handle on this thing. It's a complex project and it's going to take some time to get the results he wants. I want him to know that I can write this whitepaper and it will be good enough to go out on Carey Jones Norton letterhead."

Stan interjected. "I've got a suggestion for you."

"What's that?"

"Start your presentation just like that. Say exactly the same thing to him that you just said to me. The funny thing is that it entertains the quotation that he gave you. Simplicity on the other side of complexity seems to take time, a bit of trial and error, and some experience."

Stan paused and I jumped in. "You're right, and I can expand on it by saying that simplicity on this side of complexity is arrived at too easily and while it might sound good at first, it doesn't have the direct practical applications that he's looking for. There's a level of complexity to the simplicity on the other side of complexity and there's some learning involved because you have to move through complexity before you can discover it. He wants rock solid takeaways that the readers can implement, that's the standard he wants the whitepaper to meet."

"That sounds a lot like helping the readers get some TRaction. Somehow it always comes down to that."

"You're right again, Stan."

"So, bringing it back to you, what's on your TRaction plan today?"

"I'm still worried that I'm a little thin on real world experience at this point. I'd like to back the concepts up with some type of proof. I've been reviewing some research. I'm intrigued by the research Karl Anders Ericsson has compiled about how expertise and high performance are developed. It looks like there are some strong parallels between his body of research and the ideas that Dave has been talking about. I'm pretty sure Dave doesn't know how similar they are, but beyond that I can refer to Ericsson to demonstrate to Mr. Jones that we are on the right path." I paused for a bit as my thoughts seem to gel.

"That's really the purpose of the presentation. To show Mr. Jones that I'm on track and with some more time I'll be able to deliver a whitepaper that serves the purposes he laid out."

"That sounds great," said Stan. "I've got to get back to work but I'm looking forward to hearing more about it over lunch. I'll pick up a couple of BLTs and bring them along if that's alright with you."

"That would be awesome. I'll see you at noon and hey, Stan, thanks again. I really appreciate all your help."

"One more thing before I let you go," he said. "Dave always asks me to explain new ideas to him like I'm preparing him to explain them to a third person. He says that if I explain it to him well enough that he can make sense explaining it to somebody else, then that's when he knows I've hit the mark. I'd like to put a twist on his suggestion and ask you to explain your presentation to me with enough clarity so I can easily explain it to Dave."

"I think I've got it. My goal for our meeting at noon is to prepare you to explain the presentation to Dave. After that I'll be able to impress Mr. Jones in the meeting at 3:30."

"That's it. I'm looking forward to it. I'll see you at noon," Stan said as he hung up.

30

I checked the time. Wow, it was only 8:30 AM. This was going to be another one of those days when things moved fast.

Okay, I knew the results I wanted to achieve, I had my opening statement for the presentation, and I had a pretty good idea about what should be included.

Next I was going to review the work by Ericsson to see if I could find some more research that validates my recommendations.

I had well worn copies of *The Road to Excellence* edited by K. Anders Ericsson and *The Cambridge Handbook of Expertise and Expert Performance* edited by K. Anders Ericsson along with three other researchers. The first book is billed as a summary of the emerging knowledge of the necessary conditions for reaching international-level performance. The second book is billed as the first handbook where the world's foremost experts on expertise review their knowledge on expertise and expert performance and on how experts differ from non-experts in terms of their development, training, reasoning, knowledge, and innate talent. Both of the books were collections of well researched essays by various authors on different aspects of expertise.

I also had a stack of articles written about Ericsson's work and several reports written by the eminent researcher himself that I'd gotten off the Internet.

You'd think that what I was looking for would be easy to spot in these books and articles; however the research cut across at least fifteen different domains of expertise and unfortunately one of them wasn't business. That would be too easy. To add an extra level of difficulty the research also covered the development of expertise over the lifespan of peoples' entire careers.

I leaned back in my chair not knowing where to start. I needed to clear my mind so I thought I'd walk down to the coffee room and refill my cup. Everyone should be at their desks hard at work by now. Hopefully there wouldn't be anyone in there.

It was time to collect my thoughts. I needed to explain this research to Stan.

A few minutes away from the clutter on my desk was just what the doctor ordered. When I sat back down in front of my computer I started to work on a one pager that would concisely summarize the research.

Ericsson is on a lifelong quest to identify and articulate, to use his own words, a theoretical framework for the causal explanation of expert performance. In plain English he was searching for the true cause of high performance.

The research disputes the belief in innate ability. In field after field, from music to figure skating the evidence doesn't support the concept that certain people are born destined to be high performers. He asserts that effortful training is required for all individuals, even those who might have gifts. For the purposes of the whitepaper this essentially means that great business-people are made, not born.

Interestingly enough IQ is not a predictor of success even in intellectual fields like chess. This sounds counterintuitive but research proves that the smartest people aren't the best chess players.

He has observed that most people who get involved in an activity or project seem to stall at a level of ability and performance. Then they remain there within their comfort zones, either because they become satisfied or they just don't know how to design practice plans to move to the next level. This is similar to the next level challenge that business-people always talk about. His comprehensive review of the evidence indicates that the most successful individuals in every field engage in the most deliberate practice.

He's defined deliberate practice as being practice designed specifically to improve performance. Which I thought was a lot like company owners working on Mark's five key elements.

Engaging in deliberate practice leads to the faster accumulation of expertise and with time it also leads to eventual higher levels of performance than most others achieve. Some research indicates that it takes ten thousand hours of deliberate practice over ten years to reach the most elite world-class levels in most domains. It's important to note that most company owners do not have to reach world-class levels to achieve the success they want.

In most of the domains of expertise studied by researchers there are understood bodies of knowledge and performance levels that can be used to track and study the progress of individuals as they move through the levels. This doesn't seem to be well documented for business, but I think the five key elements would be an excellent start.

Ericsson's research also looks into the quality of the deliberate practice that high performers engage in. He breaks the overall process of the developing expertise into levels and investigates why some people's skills stall at each of the different levels. This way he can dispel the myth of innate ability and point to both the quantity and quality of deliberate practice as the reasons why or why not people continue to progress to higher levels.

Ericsson has identified some features of deliberate practice. It requires an intensity of concentration that can only be maintained for about an hour and a half at a time, it focuses on aspects of performance which means that it drills down to small details and covers all of the relevant details over time. Sounds like the CA³M and the F &V Report.

It's associated with frustrations because it is constructed to push for improvements, it is not always the most inherently enjoyable or fun activity available, there is effective feedback that is paid attention to and overall it's motivated by the eventual outcomes the participant wants. That sounds like a journey through the field of complexity.

The desired eventual results should be constantly kept in mind as motivational fuel.

I read through my summary of his work that I'd just written. It was longer than a page but it captured the essence of Ericsson. I'd been concentrating on it pretty hard. As I looked around my office I noticed that the clock on the wall read ten. It was interesting that I'd been at it for an hour and a half and it was time for a break. This must be what it feels like to go through one of his deliberate practice sessions.

The parallels between Ericsson's research and the stories Dave had been telling me were starting to become clearer. It seems that no matter what you want to get good at it needs to be broken down into achievable components and you have to move through it in a progression.

I was coming to the realization that almost anybody could build a great company if they took the right course of action, engaged in deliberate practice to strengthen their company, and didn't wind up getting stalled at one of the levels. My project was about bringing some clarity to that course of action and the content of the deliberate practice involved. That's where the five key elements come in.

I headed off to the reception desk to see how Alice was making out with the forecast and variance reports.

"Hey Alice, how's it going?"

"Not too bad. I've got the profit centers designed for both Grant and Martin's companies and I'm just working my way through their overhead cost centers now. For Grant's automotive repair business the profit centers are labor, parts, sublet, tires, and shop supplies. For Martin's plumbing business they are construction labor, service labor, materials, and fixtures. Come around to my side of the desk and have a look."

I walked around and stared at the screen for a bit. It looked like the reports were coming together but I really didn't know what to ask.

"They look good," was the only thing that I could think of to say.

"Thanks," Alice said. "It'll take me about another hour to get their overhead cost centers figured out and onto the spreadsheets. Then I'll start to transfer the numbers over to them and we'll have the first part of the forecasting done. I should have that ready in time for your meeting with Mr. Jones. I'll build the variance reports later. There's no way I can get that part ready for 3:30 today but you'll be able to take what I've got and use them to explain the rest of the concept to Mr. Jones."

"Wow, that's great," I replied.

"Thanks. I'll give you and Stan a run through before you present it to Mr. Jones."

As I walked back to my office I began to think about how I was going to use the next two hours before Stan arrived. One of the things on my list was reviewing my notes from the meeting with Dave when he described how Mark helped him to create his forecast and variance reports for Velocity Software. I could use a refresher on that.

I also needed to prepare an agenda for the presentation and get some printed materials ready so Mr. Jones could follow along more easily.

The time flew past. It seemed to be only a few minutes later when Alice appeared at my office door and announced that Stan was here waiting in the conference room. I checked the clock and sure enough it was noon, Stan arrived right on time. I gathered up my materials and headed over.

31

"Jen, it's good to see you," Stan said as I walked through the door. "Here's your BLT. I got you fries with it because I don't know what type of salad you like. I got a Caesar salad with mine. We can swap if you like."

"The fries are okay. Hey, thanks for bringing lunch. Do you want something to drink?"

"Alice is already on that; she's getting us a pitcher of water. We both think you need to slow down a bit on the coffee this afternoon," he said with a big grin on his friendly face.

It felt good to see him again. Both he and Dave had a way about them. It was a quiet confidence without any bravado. No matter how challenging or impossible things seem to me, they get me back on track and believing in myself again. I sure could use some more of that right now. There was only three and a half hours left and time was moving faster and faster.

As I unwrapped my sandwich he asked, "So where are you at now?"

"Well, I've got the agenda drafted and the backup materials ready, except for the forecast and variance reports that Alice is working on. I still need to understand them a bit better so I don't sound too clumsy in the presentation."

"Sometimes you worry too much. You're going to do well," he said.

"You have more confidence in me than I have in myself."

"Let's fix that. Can I see the agenda?"

I passed it over to him, it read:

Opening:	Review the whitepaper's purpose and parameters
Framework:	The challenges developing a framework for the project
Quote:	Review the complexity quote and discuss how it applies
Ericsson:	Review performance & expertise research —deliberate practice

Content:	The Five Key Elements as prospects for deliberate practice: Company Promise, AR²T of Momentum, Financial Information Systems, Marketing Plans and creating Accountability by using the CA³M and building systems
Next Steps:	Introduction of the above to my clients & measure progress
Q & A:	As required

"This looks good," Stan said. "Do you have a copy of the one pager that I can read while we're eating?"

"Sure do, here it is. It's actually a bit longer. That's as short as I could make it."

Stan read it as he ate his salad. At times he scratched his head and at others he rubbed his chin. I could tell that he was thinking so I didn't interrupt him. After a while he put my summary of Ericsson's work next to the agenda. Then he had the sheets spread out on the table in front of him. Alice came in and quietly placed the pitcher of water on the table in front of us.

"Thanks Alice," Stan said to her with a smile. "Okay Jen, take me through it." He reached out and poured us both a glass of water.

I started with the opening that we agreed to earlier in the morning and went through the entire presentation from start to finish. I was surprised how nervous I was at the beginning but things settled down as I got into it. There were a couple of times that I lost my train of thought. Stan gently helped me through them. All in all, it took about thirty minutes. I could see him making notes as I was speaking. I was very interested in what he was writing.

"Now it's time for the questions and answers," I said.

"I've got a few questions and some suggestions," Stan replied.

"I saw you making some notes. I hope they're not too harsh."

He laughed. "No, I just wanted to make sure that I gave you good feedback."

"What did you write down?" I asked.

"First off, I liked the words in your opening, but the tone in your voice didn't match the strength of the words. You didn't sound like you really believed them. Try it again but say it more powerfully this time, say it like you mean it."

"Okay, here it goes again," I said with all the confidence I could muster. I even used some hand motions as I went through it.

"That's better. You should probably practice it a couple of more times and it might be a good idea to tell him that you'll only need about thirty minutes of his time."

"Alright, I've got it. What else were you writing down?"

"Well, your transition from Holmes' simplicity quotation to Ericsson's research could use a bit of refinement. Developing expertise, which can also be known as discovering simplicity on the other side of complexity, appears to follow a well defined pattern that researchers have identified.

"For example, from this side of complexity there is the belief that high performers are born and not made. Under the microscope that's proving to be wrong. After extensive research a simple explanation from the other side of complexity is emerging that suggests deliberate practice is what actually leads to high performance."

"That's good. Can I use it?"

"Of course, then let him know that his instincts were right when he gave you the quotation."

"That's a beautiful little tweak."

Stan winked at me and carried on. "Really it was his idea and you should give credit where credit is due. He planted a seed with you and he expects it to grow. Keep that in mind when you're speaking to him."

He stopped, smiled, and took a sip of water. "Then you can go on with your explanation of what deliberate practice is and how you're in the process of determining what the content of it should be for owners who want to build strong companies. The five key elements certainly fit the profile."

"That really flows well, thanks," I said.

"On another note, I'm curious if any of the domains of expertise Ericsson studied involved teams or if they were all individual pursuits."

"You know, I'm a bit concerned about that too. They were all individual pursuits from what I could see."

"Also there are a lot of domains of expertise involved in building a company. If it takes ten thousand hours to be a world-class expert in all of them then you might be promoting an impossible dream."

He looked at me with a straight face and I didn't know how to answer him.

After a few seconds he couldn't hold it any longer and he laughed out loud. "Jen, you sure have a tendency to take on a lot. It seems like you're making this challenging by bringing in more issues when you're supposed to be creating simplicity by chewing on barbed wire and spitting out ball bearings."

I just looked at him for a couple of seconds trying to process what I just heard. "That's a funny way of putting it, but you're right, I've been concerned about that too," I said. "I think it's important to understand that Ericsson's research was focused on elite world-class performers. They're basically people whose goals are to become the absolute best in the world and win Olympic gold medals."

"I'm back on track with you," Stan said. "With the size of companies your whitepaper is focused on the owners' skill levels don't have to be the absolute best in the world for them to build strong companies."

Okay, I'm headed in the right direction here, I thought to myself. "Yeah, and a large portion of the ten thousand hours needed to achieve elite world-class levels are invested in a series of finer improvements after somebody is already extremely good. Our focus needs to be on accelerating the learning curve and efficiently equipping company owners so they can build strong companies. I don't think the level we're aiming at is anywhere near Ericsson's level."

"That makes sense. The finer improvements are really the domain of large companies where they can afford specialists on staff. Good examples of these would be chief financial officers or dedicated IT specialists where individuals can focus 100% of their time working in narrow fields."

"That's right," I said. "We are looking at a different part of the business growth curve where owners need to be generalists as opposed to specialists. They often have to wear a lot of hats. Then as the company grows they can delegate some of them."

"It seems like problems with any one of those hats has the potential to stall a company at any given level," said Stan. "It's like the methodology Ericsson used in his research. If I remember right, he found people who had stalled and then looked into the quality and quantity of their deliberate practice up to that point and compared it to the deliberate practice of people who had continued to progress."

"That's right. I wonder if an assessment tool could be developed for companies to help them figure it out." I made a note to look into that later. It was probably too good of an idea to pass over.

Stan's phone rang as I was about to razz him for chiding me about making things too complicated and then proceeding to introduce even more complicated stuff himself. He looked at the screen to see who it was. "It's Dave. Do you mind if I take it?"

"Not at all," I replied, nodding my head as I listened to hear what I could.

"Hey Dave, how's it going? . . . It's coming together well; we're just refining some of the details and working the bugs out . . . . You know what? I think I can explain it to you, but can you give me a few minutes and I'll call you back? . . . Thanks, talk to you soon."

Alice came in while Stan was talking to Dave. She had the forecasts with her. I glanced at the time. Only two hours to go before my big meeting.

She gave Stan a wave as she spread the forecasts out on the table in front of me. "I e-mailed them to Martin and Grant and they had some comments. They both like the way it presents the numbers but they were both disappointed with the profits that they're projected to make. All I could say was I figured out the current run rates from their statements and put them into their forecasts. If everything keep trending the same way the profits will be just like it shows here," she said, pointing to the bottom right corner of their spreadsheets.

"So they don't like them?" I asked. I was starting to get concerned again.

"That's partially true. They really like them, but they don't like the results they show."

Stan came over and looked over my shoulder at the papers on the table. "Nice work, Alice."

"What do you mean?" I asked as politely as I could.

"Well, look at the alternatives. They could work hard all year and only make that much money or they can assess these forecasts and experiment with the numbers a bit to see where they need to improve. From there they can use the AR^{2}T of momentum to make their improvements. They may not like what these forecasts are showing them, but they'll appreciate what they're doing for them. Now at least they have a fighting chance to make the profits they deserve for all the work they're going to be putting in."

"There's something else I want to mention," Alice said. "I don't mind adjusting the numbers on their forecast spreadsheets or working with their bookkeepers to make plans to revise their charts of accounts, but first we should **show them to the accountants** who do their year-ends."

"You're absolutely right Alice," I said.

"Thanks, they want to sit down with somebody and discuss them. They both mentioned that they'd like their AR^{2}T of momentum forms adjusted to reflect the changes they need to make in their companies. I'm not the right person for that."

"I'll give them a call," I said.

"I can really see how having these is a big advantage," Stan chipped in. "It's great for analyzing their business models and with the monthly variance

170

reports that Alice is creating next they'll be able to see how well their new plans come together in the real world. They'll be getting great feedback."

I wasn't saying much. I was busy trying to wrap my mind around how I was going to present this to Mr. Jones.

There was a knock on the door. Alice answered it. I could hear someone telling her that Mr. Jones was looking for her and that he seemed upset that she wasn't at the reception desk. "I have to go," she said as she hustled off.

Stan and I continued to talk about how the process of developing and using a forecast and variance report also resembled Ericsson's research. It seemed to be effective at drilling down to the finer details and identifying where companies need some deliberate practice. I was getting more and more prepared and ready for the meeting.

Alice appeared at the door again, "Hey, I've got some news," she announced.

"What's that?" I asked.

"Mr. Jones is rescheduling your meeting until Monday at three. He's working on an important client's file and doesn't want to be interrupted until it's finished."

"Not much we can do about that," I said, relieved and disappointed at the same time. "I guess we'll have to look on the bright side. It will give me more time to prepare."

Stan excused himself to call Dave. Alice headed back to her desk. It appeared that after talking with Mr. Jones she was afraid to leave it for the rest of the afternoon, even for one second. I gathered up my things.

Stan came back in and said, "Dave wants to know if you can meet with him tomorrow morning at ten."

"No problem," I said. "Where?"

He put his phone back up to his ear and repeated my question.

"The Diamond Café."

"Do you know where it is?" I asked.

"Yup, I'll give you the address," Stan replied.

We talked for a few more minutes and then he headed off to Velocity Software I went back to my office and suddenly felt all alone again.

32

I had another fitful night's sleep. Before I left Carey Jones Norton on Friday I found out that Alice had been chewed out by Mr. Jones for not being at the reception desk. I'm pretty sure it was my fault and I didn't like getting her into trouble. Every time I thought about my upcoming meeting with Mr. Jones I felt anxious.

I was still worrying the next morning as I drove towards the Diamond Café. To make matters worse it was raining, I was running late, and I was hitting every red light. I even wound up missing the turn and had to circle back.

Finally, there it was. As I pulled into the parking lot I noticed that it looked a little bit run down. I walked up to the front door and tried to imagine what it looked like twenty years ago.

When I stepped inside the first thing I saw, right in front of me, was the old cash register at home plate. The counters spread out from there, just like an infield on a ball diamond. It was exactly how Dave had described it in his story. The walls were covered with pictures of kids playing ball. Most of them looked like they'd been up there for years. I figured they might have been the same pictures that were on the walls when Dave first met Mark here.

I spotted Dave over in the right field section. He was sitting with a couple of other people at a group of tables that had been pulled together.

"Hi Dave," I said as I approached.

"Hey Jen, did you find the place all right?"

"I did get a bit lost but I'm here now," I replied, trying to sound cheerful.

"And we're happy you could join us. I thought that you'd like to meet Mark and Teru. I know that they're looking forward to meeting you."

"The pleasure is all mine," I said as I shook their hands and sat down in the chair next to Dave and across from Teru.

"When you were telling me about this place I wasn't sure if it was still here," I mentioned, trying to make conversation.

"It might not be as busy as it used to be, but it's still alive and kicking just like us," Teru commented with a smile.

"We still come down here every Saturday morning to have breakfast with the guys," Dave added.

"Really, twenty years later?"

"Yeah, you just missed the rest of the Breakfast Boys but no worries, I planned it that way. The three of us have been talking about you and your project quite a bit lately. I think Mark and Teru really want to get their two bits in on it as well. I'm also sure that they want to meet you because they don't trust me to tell the story properly."

"Either that or we thought you were making the whole thing up, that Jonsie has always been a pain in the arse, even when he was a kid," Mark said grumpily.

Everybody laughed. Mark was sitting in a wheelchair at the end of the table across from Dave. It looked to me that Mark was well into his eighties now but I sensed that he had a much younger spirit.

"Do you guys still have that same routine where you take turns buying for the whole table?" I asked.

"Yeah, but I don't think Teru has bought once in the last five years," Mark chipped in again with his deadpan manner.

They all laughed again and Teru put up a bit of defence. I could tell that it was all in good fun. It was easy to see that they liked each other.

"We wanted to meet you," Teru said, "because Mark has a few things he wants to say. I should warn you that he's a bit crusty nowadays."

I looked over at Mark and he was smiling. I was getting the distinct impression that he enjoyed being grumpy and it was plainly obvious that he was good at it.

"What is it you want to say, Mark?" I asked.

"I like your directness," he replied. "Mostly it's that knowing and doing are two completely different things. That's what I see. You know back when I was coaching ball I didn't just walk out there at the first practice of the season and demonstrate how to field a grounder and then expect the kids to do it perfectly for the rest of the season. It takes some repetition for them to get good at it. Even then you have to repeat it every once in a while to make sure bad habits don't creep back in."

"That's a good point."

"It's the same in business only harder. Over the years I helped a lot of people build their companies. Some of them get it, like Dave here, but other folks are just too addicted to doing business. They'll give you all kinds of excuses as to why they don't have time to practice, as you and that Ericsson guy put it. Those are the people that will never have any time for anything else either because the business will own them instead of them owning their company."

He paused before continuing. "For example, you can't just do a forecast and then expect business to get better. That's just the start. You need to carry on, get the variances and drill into them. Then make your changes and move on to creating the next year's forecast that's a reasonable stretch all over again. It takes at least a year to get good at it. There are lots of people who only want to work on stuff that they can get good at easily but, I've watched them struggle for years because of that mindset. Consistently profitable companies take some effort to build."

"Tell us how you really feel," Dave interrupted.

Everybody laughed again.

Mark continued. "You can lead a horse to water but you can't make them drink is what people say. I think that it's a bit more accurate to say: it's easier to act your way into a new way of thinking than it is to think your way into a new way of acting."

"Look out, here comes TRaction again," Teru said as he winked to me, then he turned to Mark. "I know you invented the AR²T of momentum but don't you think we've heard it enough about it already?"

Mark cut him off. "That's exactly the point I'm trying to make here! People have to act on it and it takes more than one swing on the gate."

Dave looked over at me. "Some of Mark's sayings are a little tough to follow."

"I got that one," I said as I was trying to wrap my mind around how I'd wound up here. It seemed like time stopped at the Diamond Café twenty years ago. Had I fallen into some type of mysterious time vortex?

"You know, I thought that this place would be busier. You told me how special the Diamond was."

"When Doug retired he sold it to the Changs. They were new to the country and didn't speak the language very well. They had a tough time integrating themselves into the community because of it. On top of that they never played ball so they don't understand the game. A big part of the customer base has slowly drifted away. Now they're a bit short on profits and can't keep up with the maintenance like Doug used to."

"It's too bad," Teru said. "I help them out where I can but they don't have much money for materials."

"When you don't know the language it's hard to be curious and that was Doug's magic ingredient," Mark added. "If you know the language, you can develop effective curiosity just the same as you can develop any other skill. They just started too far behind and couldn't catch up when the new fangled restaurants moved into town."

Dave jumped back into the conversation. "This used to be a place where everybody knew your name and now we live in a town full of restaurants where nobody knows your name. Some types of progress are actually steps backwards in my opinion."

"You're right on there," Teru said. "Jen, there is another piece of the puzzle that Mark wants to add. He'll have to do it straightaway because he's due back at the rest home pretty quick. The nurses will miss his charming personality and they'll probably file a missing person report if I don't get him back by eleven." The sound of their laughter filled the cafe again.

"Especially that Cathy, I think she's got an eye for me," Mark quipped.

After some more friendly banter between them he carried on. "There are two pieces I want to talk about actually. The first one comes from Benjamin Bloom who studied this type of stuff long before Ericsson. It's important to me because it's the foundation of the league. Our slogan has always been 'Everybody Wins' because the main goals are for the kids to learn, have fun, and to help get them on the right track for leading a good life. Winning games and trophies are just byproducts."

Teru piped up. "When the adults become overly focused on winning games it brings a whole other dynamic in and then the league doesn't work as well for the kids."

"I always thought that winning was part of the fun," Dave chirped.

"Hey ladies, I was talking here," Mark growled in a strangely friendly way.

I couldn't help but think that I should have brought my notebook. Their conversation sounded like it was ready to descend into chaos at any given moment and I wanted to remember the important parts.

After a bit more chatter, Mark got back on track again. "Bloom identified three domains of educational objectives. They were cognitive, psychomotor, and affective, which basically means thinking, physical, and emotions. He studied them in depth and wrote books that are widely considered to be some of the most influential works on the subject of learning in the twentieth century."

Teru and Dave were nodding along now.

"Anyways, people didn't like the overly fancy words so over time it was getting presented as knowledge, attitudes, and skills, or KAS for short. I never liked that arrangement, so I changed it to ASK: attitude, skills, and knowledge. I always thought that attitude should come first, then you get the kids practicing skills and from there they would naturally pick up the knowledge more easily."

I felt that I should say something. "That makes an incredible amount of sense to me."

"Every once in a while I come up with a good idea and that was one of them. We drilled that into the kids, coaches, umpires, volunteers and parents. If you want to learn something ASK. Show up with the right attitude, be prepared to practice your skills and you'll gain the knowledge you need. Asking good questions along the way is using curiosity and it sure speeds up the process."

"That's a neat little package," I mumbled half to myself.

"It works really well in business," Dave chimed in. "A lot of companies hire employees based on their experience and then take the attitude that comes with it. Instead they should develop policies, systems, and training plans. Then hire for attitude and develop people that they really want to have in their companies."

Mark looked a little annoyed by being interrupted. "There's more to Bloom's work than that but we didn't get overly technical with the kids. If we could get the basics across to them I was happy, as long as I could get them to also see that curiosity is a skill too. Curiosity is the magic ingredient in ASK. It's the like the yeast that makes the bread rise. Nobody else is going to teach them that curiosity is central to learning and it's at the very core of all relationships too. It adds spice to life."

That caught my attention. "Really, it's at the core of relationships?"

"Sure. Let me ask you this: if somebody doesn't want to know anything about you or what's going on in your life, how important does that make you feel?"

"Not very important I suppose." I never thought about it that way before.

"The trick is learning to set your curiosity at the right level. Your close relationships should have more and people like your dentist should have less. When you learn to be genuine with it, you'll have lots of friends. Asking too many questions isn't good and asking questions when you don't care about the answers isn't good either so you have to find the right balance with everybody."

Mark stopped talking and looked a little confused as to what to say next.

Teru turned to me. "The ASK acronym reminds me to think about questions that should be coming to my mind. What would be interesting to know more about? That's curiosity in a nutshell. Some practice makes it easier to have good questions where ever you go, whatever you do, whoever you meet. I guess you and Ericsson would call that deliberate practice."

"Wow, this is neat stuff," I said, praying that I could remember it I was thinking curiosity could be a candidate for the sixth element.

"Yeah, we put our own spin on Bloom's work and so did a lot of other people but sometimes there was a problem with it," Mark said. He seemed to be back with us now.

"What's that?" I asked curious myself now.

"That's the second thing that I wanted to talk about it. We noticed that some of the kids still weren't learning and this lead us to discover a missing piece. It was something called self efficacy. The theory originated with Albert Bandura, one of the most influential psychologists in history."

Dave and Teru hadn't said anything for a while and I noticed that they were looking at me as if to see whether or not I was curious and paying attention. I said to Dave, "I would have liked to make notes."

He smiled. "No worries, he's told us this a thousand times and we can tell it better than he can now. If you have any questions just call."

Mark shook his head and said, "The older you get, the worse your attitude gets, young man."

"Maybe we're catching that from you!" said Teru.

They all laughed again.

"Anyways, I'm sure the lovely young lady would like to hear me finish. So if you could be quiet for just a few more minutes, I know she'll appreciate it," Mark said in a falsely dignified voice.

He cleared his throat and, acting in a haughty manner for dramatic effect, he continued. "Self efficacy really boils down to individual's own self-perceptions about how they will be able to perform."

"I like to think of them as self-expectations. Expectations are a lot closer to core beliefs than they are to thoughts. Our thoughts automatically adjust to be in line with our core beliefs."

"You're right, Mark. We don't come up with many thoughts that run counter to our beliefs."

"That's right, Jen. To continue, if you expect to you'll be able to perform then your chances are much better. You'll deal with any obstacles and roadblocks that you encounter. On the other hand, when somebody stops expecting to be able to get results then they get off the horse whether it's dead or not."

"Stay with him here," Teru said. "It takes a while for the light bulb to go on but this touches every aspect of people's lives. People's expectations are mostly based on their own opinions regarding their own previous experiences and they come into play before the mind even has a chance to start producing thoughts. Expectations have a huge influence on our ability to learn, they also heavily impact all the life choices people make and they virtually determine whether or not people are resilient in the face of adversity."

"And that's just the tip of the iceberg," Dave said. "You can feel yourself learning, making good choices, and being resilient, but it is very difficult to see any negative self efficacy expectations that you have. You can only look for clues and learn how to read them and to do that you need to put yourself into new and challenging situations."

"That's why we built the batting cage," said Teru. "It's our temple."

Mark cut in trying to take control of the conversation again. "Teru's right. It's often said that batting is the toughest thing to do in all of sports. Even good hitters fail more often than they succeed. A batting average of .333 is pretty respectable and that amounts to failing twice for every time you succeed."

He motioned for the server to fill his glass of water and I held up my coffee cup for a refill. This morning was a real adventure for me. If you'd have told me a six months ago that I'd be here with three old guys listening with my full attention, I wouldn't have believed you.

"Okay, so I'm curious about everything you guys are saying here, but can I ask a strange question? Why do you call the batting cage your temple?"

"That's an easy one. We should let Mark take it!" Teru chimed.

"You're a bit cheeky my friend," he replied before turning to me. "The batter's box during a game is a pressure packed place for kids to be. Everybody at the diamond is looking at you, you're in direct competition with the pitcher, an umpire is judging your decisions, your team is depending on you, and on top of that there's a distinct possibility that you might swing and miss. You can even get hit by a wild pitch and if you strike out the walk back to the dugout is no picnic either."

"All of that makes it a great place to observe efficacy," Dave said.

"What does that have to do with the batting cage being your temple?"

"That's where we build efficacy in the kids," Dave responded. "Let me put it this way: trying to teach math to kids who don't think they are any good at it is a real challenge. You may as well throw the whole ASK concept right out the door and beat your head on the frame. The students are not going to participate long enough to engage in the learning process. Bandura recognized that it's not likely to work until you raise their level of efficacy. Put another way, if you help them expect to succeed first and get them believing in themselves it will be like working with a completely different group of kids. You have to find a way to prove to them that they can be good at math and then you'll be amazed at how much faster they learn."

"I'm still with you but I'm not there yet," I said.

"The batting cage is where we build efficacy. The machine is not trying to beat them. We set the speed where they can handle it. There is no umpire. Hardly anybody is watching. If they swing and miss the ball, they don't strike out. The team is not depending on them and compared to games they get a month's worth of pitches in fifteen minutes. Our primary job in there is to get them believing they can swing the bat and hit the ball. It's all about them believing in themselves on a deep down level. 'Everybody Wins' lives in there."

"I get it now!"

Mark smiled and said, "It's a good thing that you're young. It's a long road that you're on."

"What's that?" I asked, a bit confused by his remark.

"Don't worry about it," Dave said. "He didn't mean anything negative by it. It's just his way, and speaking of that, Teru and Mark should be on their way now or they're going to be late."

Teru stood up and put on his jacket and started pushing Mark's wheelchair towards the door. "It was good to meet you and I hope we can do it again soon," they said as they waved and headed on their way.

Dave looked over at me and asked, "Can you stay for a few more minutes?" I nodded. "I'll be right back. It's quite the production getting Mark into Teru's pickup. We have to get a box out for him to step up on and then steady him as he gets into the truck. He lets out a rank little fart almost every time. Teru thinks he does it on purpose, but I don't think that he can help it. If I'm not there they'll create such a disturbance that someone might call the cops." He quickly got up and hustled off towards the door after them.

33

I was fretting about Mark's remark as I moved my chair around to where his wheelchair had been so I'd be sitting across from Dave when he returned. A couple more people came into the café. The server separated our grouping of six tables.

I thought that she must have been the Changs' daughter. She didn't say anything and she seemed to be very shy. I waved at her. She gave me a little smile back.

When Dave returned and sat down, right away I asked, "What did Mark mean by that comment? Does he think I'm stupid?" I sounded more brisk than I intended and immediately regretted my tone.

Mark looked right at me. He held his gaze for a couple of seconds and then his face broke into a grin.

"Now that he's older he's more inclined to say exactly what comes to his mind without thinking about it too much beforehand," he paused for a bit. "I'm sure you want to know what he actually meant."

I squeaked a quick "yeah" out of my mouth.

"The project you're working on is about what he did for a living. Probably the only regret that he has in life is not documenting it. He could have had a much larger reach and made a bigger impact. He's actually pretty excited about you coming along, but based on his own personal experience he expects that it's going to take you a while. That's what he meant when he said it was a good thing that you're young. Now, if he said that it was a good thing you were young and pretty he'd be right on both counts, but in that case he probably would have been insulting you at the same time," Dave laughed at his own joke.

I felt my face warming up. "This breakfast is not for the thin skinned is it?"

"Not by any stretch. However I've always been able to count on having them in my corner when I needed them. When I look up loyalty in the dictionary I see their pictures."

I let out a sigh of relief. Anxious to change the subject I said, "He seemed okay. I remember you telling me that senility was getting him. Is he getting better?"

"No, but he's not too bad in the mornings. As the day wears on it gets harder for him. If the nurses can limit the amount of activity around him and get him down for a nap or two then he's okay for some afternoons, but you wouldn't believe it was the same person when the sun goes down. It's called Sundowners Syndrome. They don't know how to treat it and they aren't even sure exactly what causes it. It just happens to some people when they get old and Mark drew a bum hand on this one."

A look of sadness flashed over Dave's face. "We got him into a suite in The West Valley Gardens that looks out over the ballpark, but the nurses tell us we'll probably have to move him to the other side of the building pretty soon. Even seeing a game under the lights is getting to be too much for him to handle."

Dave took a couple of deep breaths and then continued. "Before I go and get all misty on you I should get back on track. I also want to tell you about marketing plans. That seems to be a hole in your presentation for Jones. If you've got an hour or so to spare I'll go over them with you."

"That sounds good. Thanks very much."

"Ok, I brought you a pen and some paper from my car," Dave said as he slid them towards me.

"Thanks again."

"Marketing plans have a singular purpose. They should be designed to connect the company with customers who are ideally suited to it. A marketing plan is the bridge that connects your company to the people who can benefit from your company promise and appreciate the value it delivers."

"Is this like Teru's Irish farmer story?" I asked.

"That's right Jen. Starting from the right place is important and it's harder to do than you might think. There are a lot of people out there selling advertising to companies and it can be tempting to start with whoever comes through the door next. They all tell you that their product will do wonderful things, but none of them offer guarantees. It's easy to chew through a marketing budget without getting the results you think you're paying for."

"How do you deal with that?"

"Well, when company owners are developing marketing plans there are six challenges that they need to consider. I suggest they consider them before they start to spend any money, if they can."

"What are they?"

"I'll take you through them. Always remember that it's the customers who own the business, so it's crucial that your marketing offers them benefits they'll buy into. That's the **first challenge**: benefits they'll buy into. If you don't have benefits that enough people will buy into then you really need to look long and hard in a mirror and re-evaluate your company promise."

"Let's say your company promise isn't off the mark. How do you go about figuring out the benefits they'll buy into?" I asked.

"That's a great question. To get the answer let's think about Grant at West Valley for a minute. Let me start by asking you a question. What's the difference between a customer and a client?"

His question caught me by surprise. I hadn't thought of it before. "I'm not sure. Why's that important?'

"Well, I know I haven't told you this before and sometimes even I get sloppy and don't use the words properly, but customers are transactional in nature. By that I mean vending machines have customers. You put the money in and you get the soda out. When you have a client there is an implied duty of care that extends beyond the transaction and it's highly likely there's an ongoing relationship involved. To put a finer line on it, I buy coffee regularly at Starbucks, but I'm not a client, I'm just another regular customer. There's no ongoing duty of care and having one fundamentally changes the nature of the relationship from customer to client."

"Okay, but again, why is that important?"

"I didn't mention it before, but from what you told me Grant is trying to wrap his mind around a good company promise. Reading between the lines I hear that he wants client relationships to be a central part of it. He's ready and willing to accept a duty of care for his clients' vehicles."

"I think you're right."

"In a roundabout way that brings me back to your question. The benefits his potential customers will buy into are different from the benefits his potential clients will buy into. The client buy-in is likely more challenging for Grant, particularly if they've had no way of knowing each other beforehand. A better way to build his client base might be to market to customers where he can get easier buy-in. Then run a second marketing strategy that converts his customers into clients. If the first experience is good then the client buy-in will be easier."

"That makes sense."

"A friend of mine in Canada built a small chain of gas fireplace stores because he understood that the reason people initially chose to purchase a gas fireplace was different from the reason they chose the particular fireplace they actually wound up buying. His marketing plan recognized this and worked with the changing buy-in. In a highly competitive market he did very well. His stores consistently got more than their fair share of the market."

"With a healthy helping of curiosity, a little common sense, a dash of intuition, and some experimentation it's possible to discover what the buy-ins are for any market. It's a perfect application for ASK. You'll always know when you're on the right track because that's when you'll be getting the right kind of business coming your way."

The Changs' daughter came by our table again and asked if we wanted anything else. Mark switched to water and thanked her. That's when I found out her name was Nora. I ordered a toasted egg sandwich mostly because I could eat it and still take notes at the same time. The restaurant was almost empty now. Only two of the front booths were taken and there was a couple of kids were sitting on the infield stools chattering away.

Mark waited for me to turn back towards him before he started talking again.

"We're sitting in the middle of a great example. Doug and Julie were masters of curiosity about buy-ins and this place was always full. Now the Changs' curiosity is blocked by a language barrier and Nora is pretty shy. To top it off the Diamond was obviously built for ball fans and they've never played the game. The place is barely hanging on mostly because curiosity is missing."

"I see what you mean," I said. It was really obvious and the difference it made was amazing.

"The **second challenge** a marketing plan has to consider is resistance. If you have benefits and there isn't any resistance then you should get the business, but it's almost never that easy. Resistance is normally part of the equation and it comes in all shapes and sizes. A good marketing plan is curious about resistance and develops strategies to minimize it."

"Resistance and objections are the same, aren't they? I've read about them."

"That's a good thought, but it's not quite right. I don't believe in objections. They're just the excuses that people give for not buying. They give objections because they either don't want the benefits enough to pay for them or there's resistance somewhere. The problem with focusing on objections is that a fair amount of the time they're just excuses that don't match the real problem.

"I remember a saying that my daughter Ann had as the screensaver on her computer back when she left for university on her softball scholarship:

183

If you want something bad enough you'll find a way,
if not you'll find excuses.

"She used that saying to motivate herself and it worked. When you look at it from a different angle it also applies to objections. If you're getting objections it means the customer's buy-in isn't strong enough or their resistance is stronger. Those are the problems you really need to solve. Objections are the excuses that people come up with. Sometimes they're genuine, but quite often they're just phantom symptoms that don't match the real problems.

"At Velocity Software we're well aware of the resistance to change, the resistance to the unknown, and the resistance to the time commitment. Price plays into it too, but we can easily justify that. If we can't then we shouldn't be after that piece of business anyways. It's the other types of resistance that are our bigger issues. Our marketing plan is designed to address them.

"In other cases resistance might be caused by a competitive offering that's better suited to them. It could also be something you really don't expect. For example, a prospect could be tight on cash because they have a leaky roof that needs to be replaced. In instances like these many prospects have been known to tell companies that their price is too high. I'm rambling a bit, but I've seen too many companies drop their prices lower than their business model can afford simply because they've heard the price excuse way too often. One more thing while I'm on my high horse: I've heard that about 12% of people shop on price and price alone. They actually appear to be a much larger group than they really are, mostly because they're in the habit of price checking a lot of companies. They shop around more than other people do."

"I have a friend like that and you're right, she does a lot of shopping before she buys anything," I said.

Nora put the sandwich in front of me. I thanked her and took a bite. I'd forgotten how hungry I was; it tasted delicious.

Mark continued. "So as your marketing plan develops you get to know the benefits they'll buy in too and you understand how to deal with the different types of resistance you're going to encounter. The **third challenge** is initiating contact and exchanging information."

"Exchanging information. Are we asking them out on a date?" I chipped in cheekily.

"That's a good analogy, actually. I'm sure there are things you'd like to know before you go on a date with somebody and there are things customers would like to know before they do business with a company. There are even things they'd like to know before they pick up the phone and call or maybe even before they drop by the company's place of business to find out more. Some people want to know more than others so your material should be presented in a way that works for the full range of shoppers. It really helps to think this through in the planning stage."

"How do you do that?" I asked.

"It's a good idea to grab a system template and try and write out the system customers are using to buy your type of products and services."

"Dave, they might follow a pattern, but I'm sure they're not even aware of it themselves. Won't that make it difficult to write a system out?" I asked. It seemed a bit farfetched to me.

"I agree it's not easy and you probably won't get it right the first time, but—and this is a really big but—if you keep working at it in a couple of years it'll be one of the most valuable documents your company owns. It will keep you right on top of how your market is behaving. You might even find that there are two or three systems that different groups of customers are using. Those systems are also known as buyers' cycles and a strong marketing plan works in harmony with them.

"You can also think about it as building your credibility with the clients or customers. Some types of purchases need more credibility than others. Software is a good example. Part of what they're trying to figure out is whether or not we can do the job and deliver on our company promise. They really want to know if they're actually going to get what they pay for. A marketing plan should have a pretty good idea about how much credibility is needed and when it's needed in the buying cycle."

It occurred to me that it wouldn't make sense for a marketing plan to go against Dave's advice here. He's a master of the obvious. It's just that a lot of things only become obvious to me after he tells me about them.

"Here's something that will help you remember this. A marketing plan is the bridge to your ideal clients. If they find it challenging to pedal their buy cycle over your bridge you're not likely to get their business. That's a real problem and your company will experience some nasty symptoms because of it."

I laughed out loud and Dave couldn't help himself, he laughed too.

"Okay, here we go again. There's more good stuff I need to tell you about marketing, but first I want to make the point that with different types of customers using different buyers' cycles and companies often selling into more than one market it means that bridges often works best with a number of lanes on them."

"I think we're in the field of complexity again," I said.

"There's no doubt about it, but you have to go through there to discover the simplicity that most business-people would give their lives for. I think now you've got a better understanding about how to navigate through it. Your man Ericsson would tell you that some time needs to be invested in deliberate practice. I'm here laying out the six challenges that comprise the practice plan for marketing. Mark would remind you of ASK. He'd tell you that you need to be curious, have the right attitude and work with it some to develop your skills and grow your knowledge. Benjamin Bloom would also remind you to look for some early wins to build your efficacy."

I laughed at him again. I'm not sure why, but I did.

He smiled back. "When Oliver Wendell Holmes said he'd give his life for simplicity on the other side of complexity, I'm pretty sure he knew that it wasn't just the simplicity that would be different. I think he expected that he would have to learn and grow as he moved through the complexity to discover the simplicity on the other side. And just like Ericsson I think he knew that the journey wouldn't always be easy."

"I expect you're right."

"According to Ericsson it will take an organized practice plan and 10,000 hours of work for someone to become a world-class golfer. After that they'll easily be able to hit a 200 yard shot over water onto a green and make it look simple."

"I'm with you here, but where are we headed with this?"

Dave had a big grin on his face. "Nowadays that golfer is only about twenty five years old and he pretty much has given his life for simplicity on the other side of complexity."

"So what you're trying to tell me is marketing is not that much different?"

"It shouldn't take anywhere near as much time to build a great marketing plan, but it follows the same principles. You need a deliberate practice plan that effectively leads you through the field of complexity or learning zone. Then as you do the work the simplicity you're after will emerge."

"Why are you telling me this again? Am I missing something?"

"I just want to make a point. The same pattern applies to all of the five key elements. The readers of your whitepaper need to clearly see the practice plans and work them right through to simplicity. If they don't, they might start believing that business is too complex for them to understand or worse yet they could start believing their own excuses, which strangely enough might not match the real problems with their company. Then they'll have low efficacy."

"No question about that."

"Okay, let's get back to marketing. We talked about the information exchange from the customers' point of view. On the flip side the company needs to know what the customers are interested in and if their business is a good fit for the company. Chasing dragons can use up a lot of energy and companies can get burned even worse if they catch them. A company should have some key questions lined up in advance. Kind of like a curiosity plan. Actually no, it should be a curiosity plan. You want to make sure that you're putting your effort into the right prospects.

"Collecting the prospects particulars is also important, including their name, address, e-mail, phone number, or website. It all helps to build the database."

"Isn't that hard to do? I remember Ray at the St. John Pub saying it was hard to get e-mail addresses even from his regular customers."

"It's easy, all you have to do is give them a reason that they can buy into. Ray could say he'll e-mail them a coupon for a free drink on their birthday every year. Then he can send it out a week in advance. Hopefully they'll come down with a bunch of their friends and he'll turn nice profit on the deal. Grant can offer the same deal with an oil change. Not as high a percentage will be able to come in on their actual birthday so it likely won't cost him full pop, but I'll bet that he still gets their e-mail addresses."

I thought about it for a minute. "Grant can do that on a one-time basis too. He can offer it just to his new customers for their next birthday."

"That's right and there are other good ideas too that relate more directly to the business at hand and don't need an incentive. For example, can we e-mail you the invoice so you have an electronic copy? The key is, if you want to build your database you have to have a reason for the right people to give you their information. If you don't supply a reason, you won't get very far. The reason has to have buy-in of its own and it should be developed as part of the marketing plan. Then you need to make it a priority and make sure your people are trained to be in the habit of following through."

Dave was a master of the obvious once again.

"Initiating contact is always interesting. I like to think of it as hunting, fishing, and farming. Hunting is when you know what your future customers and clients look like and you market out directly to them. Fishing is using mass media, it's when you drop your net into the ocean and hope to catch customers and clients. Farming is when you're working your database for business."

"Can you expand on that for me?"

"Sure. Think back to the system you developed for Velocity. That's hunting. We have a limited number of prospects and we have a very good idea about how to find them. We market to groups of them at once, but everything is individualized for each prospect.

"If I remember correctly Martin at Hydro Plumbing is building his renovation and service work by buying Google Adwords and taking out advertisements in local papers. That's fishing because he's sending his ads out to the world or dropping his net into the ocean if you will.

"Grant at West Valley Auto likely has the addresses of his clients and I suspect he mails service reminders and specials out to them, that's farming his database. He also does some fishing with his advertising, but his location is his biggest net by far. Maybe Ron Waltham could help improve his results there with some better signage."

"Didn't the Velocity system also involve sending case studies to your database?"

"Well, you're right it's not a pure hunting system anymore, but almost every name in our database originally came from hunting. Farming is less costly and less work to boot so over the years we've put a lot of energy into growing our database. There are a lot of companies that use hunting and farming to get business and grow their database at the same time. If it's clean and built right the database is the most valuable asset a company owns. Looking again at Grant's company, his end game is to build a large database of clients. When he's got that done West Valley's profitability will be almost guaranteed."

Nora came by our table again. I got a refill, Dave stayed with water. I noticed that the kids in the infield were gone. The Diamond was almost empty now.

"There's also organic growth to consider. Having a strong company promise and consistently delivering it will lead to referrals and repeat business. With many companies this is their best source of new business, but you still need some marketing to get the ball rolling."

"You're right. A referral strategy should be part of a marketing plan."

"Jen, I've got another question for you. The last time you referred someone to a company, who were you mainly trying to help out, the customer or the company? You have to pick one or the other."

I thought for a bit. "I'd like to say both, but it was the customer I was helping out."

"Over eighty percent of the time I ask that question—the answer is the customer. I'll tell you why that's interesting. Generally most people give referrals because they feel good about helping somebody or they feel good about sharing what they know. If I offer you money to refer customers to Velocity Software then you'll be doing it for yourself. It won't feel right. It won't be altruistic anymore. Getting paid ruins the feeling for a lot of people."

"That's interesting."

"That's why companies have a hard time ramping up their best source of business. My suggestion is for the companies to give a little something extra to the customer who is being referred. Grant could give free windshield wipers for example. Then when you suggest to a friend that they go to West Valley Auto you can also tell them to say that you sent them and they'll get a free set of windshield wipers—won't you feel good then?"

"Sure and I'll probably send a lot more people too."

"Isn't that a great way to initiate contact? It works with the altruistic psychology behind referrals. Grant also shouldn't forget to say thank you. Doing you a small favor somewhere down the road wouldn't hurt either.

"At this point in the marketing plan it's time to bring out an annual calendar where you can see all your initiatives in one place. Then schedule in your hunting, fishing, and farming activities. Put your expected costs on it too."

"That's a good idea, getting it all laid out so you can visualize it."

"Initiating contact is your prospects end of the bridge. The question you have to be asking yourself is: will the marketing plan contact enough of the right kind of people the right way? You don't want to build a bridge to nowhere. Sometimes I see companies spend a lot of their marketing dollars on a fancy website, but where's the contact? I'm not saying it's wrong. It could turn out to be a great investment with some search engine optimization, ad words on Google, and maybe even Facebook ads to support it as well, but it's the contact that's important."

"You were saying it had to contact people the right way. What did you mean by that?" I asked.

Dave got a big grin on his face. "Are you ready for doughnut marketing?"

I just shook my head, smiled, raised my hands, and said, "Whatever. Bring it on."

"Okay, get a fresh sheet of paper and draw a three inch circle in the middle and a six inch circle around that."

"This looks a lot like the leaning zone diagram we drew the first time I met you."

"Yup and you're going to learn something right now," he said with a big grin on his face.

"Inside the first circle write 'expected'. Then inside the second circle write 'unexpected'. Then outside the circles write 'too far gone'."

I drew the diagram and pushed the paper out to the middle of the table. It looked like a doughnut.

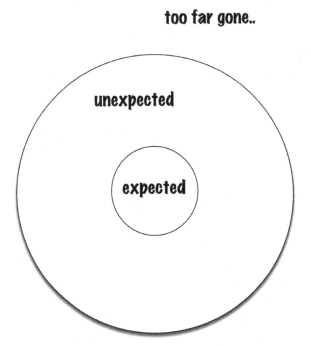

too far gone..

unexpected

expected

"In the expected circle is where you see the common type of marketing that almost every company in the market sends out. In Grant's case it might be an oil change special, with Ray it might be a happy hour special, with Martin if might be 10% off a service call, or it could say he's got twenty-four hour service. Ben at ABC Landscaping could flier a neighbourhood with a price for weeding and cutting. If it looks the same as everybody else selling into the market, it goes in the inner circle.

"These approaches generate some business, but good marketing gets into the unexpected in some way. For example, it's pretty much generally accepted that the 'Where's the Beef' commercials by Wendy's were some of the best television commercials of all time. That's because nobody really expected an old lady to look at a competitor's hamburger and yell, 'Where's the beef?' They're not your typical fast food commercials. They cut through the clutter to get the right audience's attention and they made the benefits of Wendy's hamburgers obvious."

"I've seen those ads, they're great."

"They initiated contact in a way that got the right people's attention the right way. That's a winning combination. Everyone has a lot of marketing messages coming at them every single day. It takes something unexpected to cut through and get attention. Some creativity and experimenting here go a long way."

I looked at the paper and the doughnut reference was obvious. "What about the too far gone part of the page?"

Dave started to chuckle. "Well, the best marketing ideas are further out in the dough, but if you push it too far it backfires. The second circle is the limit that you can go before it loses effectiveness. Let's say the same Wendy's ad was done with a middle aged woman who took a bite of the competitor's hamburger, chewed it, then spit it out on the floor and yelled 'Nothing but bun', then the commercial likely would have been a flop. It still would have been unexpected, but it would have gone too far."

"The moral of the story is to keep your marketing between the circles. That's when you'll be in the dough!"

I laughed. "Where did you get this stuff?"

He smiled. "It started with Mark, but believe it or not I actually came up with some of it on my own. Marketing has been one of my main roles at Velocity for a while now and I've put a fair amount of thought into it. I want to make sure I do it well and pass it along before I sell the company to the employees. But you haven't heard the best part yet. It's the big finish and it's coming pretty soon."

"I can't wait."

"The **fourth challenge** is delivering some value along with your message. It could be something as simple as a sheet of questions that the customers should be asking when they're buying your product. This works well in unusual purchases."

"What's an unusual purchase?" I asked.

"It's something that people probably will only buy once or twice in their lives. Flooring, a furnace, shocks for a vehicle, plumbing for a renovation, a sign for a new company location, and even a new accountant are examples. The identifying feature of unusual purchases is that the customer isn't familiar with their own buy cycle and they likely feel they're at a disadvantage. The first time somebody buys software is another good example. Anyways, if you help them learn about a good buy cycle they'll feel more in control and appreciate it. Plus it gives you the opportunity to tune their buy cycle so it turns towards your company."

Dave chuckled and then made a motion like he was steering a bicycle. I could tell that he'd used this idea successfully before.

"There's all kind of other ways you can add value. Finding ones that are effective does a couple of very useful things. First it invokes the Law of Reciprocity which basically means people want to return the favour. You do something nice for me and I'll want to do something nice for you, which hopefully is them giving you their business. Second when you deliver some value to them they're more likely to keep engaging in the conversation and take the time to look at your future marketing pieces. These are early relationship building strategies"

"So we're back to relationships?" I asked playfully.

Dave laughed. "Well, would you go out with somebody who was narcissistic?"

"Not if I knew," I said.

"You'd be amazed at how many companies market like narcissists. Everything is always about themselves. Marketing plans always work better when you mix in some kind of value. It could be direct value for them in their buy cycle or some collateral value that they'll appreciate. It shows that you're not just self interested."

"That makes sense."

"Think about the Diamond for a second. They still cook whole turkeys nowadays and not many people know about it. They could have a special and advertise it. They could also put tips about how to cook a turkey on their website and maybe even put their turkey soup recipe up there too. It's awesome. The Changs could also come up with some other ways to initiate contact around it. Here's the beauty of it. People don't cook turkeys very often, so they obviously can't make the soup very often. If they like it as much as I do, they'll want to have it for lunch more often than they can actually make it. Then they'll know where to come and get it. That's just one idea to get you thinking about the concept."

"It's getting near lunchtime, maybe I'll stay for the turkey soup," I said, smiling.

"The Diamond has an effect on some people and I see you're catching the bug. You better be careful, it's hard to get rid of."

"I think I can handle it," I replied, but I wasn't so sure.

"This challenge is about delivering some value with your message. We haven't talked much about the message yet. It can get lost pretty easily. Over the years a lot of people have asked me to help them with their marketing. My first question is always: What do you want people to know about your company? Next I ask to look at the marketing that they've been doing and their answer is hardly ever there. It's surprising because that's the message they should be getting out. It should be a thread running through all of their marketing initiatives."

"Really, that many people miss that? It doesn't make sense."

"I know, but it happens way more often than you think. That's why this is placed this far down in the challenges. It's checking to make sure the essential message isn't missing for the marketing plan."

"Okay let's keep moving. The **fifth challenge** is getting feedback. Most companies particularly at the size your whitepaper is concentrating on don't track where their customers come from. That means they only have a vague idea about what's bringing them in.

"Let's go back to Grant at West Valley Auto. I would be great if he knew how many customers call in or stop because of his advertisements. Then he could see how his different ads are producing and use the feedback to improve the design his ads in the future. He could also experiment with different advertising mediums to see if he gets better results there.

"There's another level to the feedback. You also want to know what percentage of the people who call or drop by actually become customers. Plus you want to know about the potential lifetime value of the customer. Some customers only buy the screaming specials while others go on to become great clients. Different initiatives often attract different qualities of buyers. Quantity doesn't always tell you the whole picture."

"You're right," I said. "You were talking earlier about Mark and Phil giving feedback to the ball players and how it made them better. I know that same process isn't being used effectively in most small companies, which is surprising for something as important as their marketing."

"Before you complete a marketing plan you should clearly know why you're doing the things you're doing. You should also know how you're going to track and monitor the plan's initiatives to determine if they're getting the expected results, or not. That way you can keep improving year after year. Great marketing plans are developed through a series of experiments that keep building on each other."

"That's a great way to think about it," I said.

"There's one last thing before the big finish."

"That's good," I said as ran my thumb over my pages of notes. Wow there was a lot there. My fingers were starting to hurt from writing so much.

"The **sixth challenge** in a marketing plan is evaluating the return on investment, or ROI. There's a quotation that's often attributed to John Wanamaker.

> Half the money I spend on advertising is wasted;
> the trouble is I don't know which half.

"I've heard that one before."

"It's a fairly famous saying and it makes a valid point. Measuring ROI can be difficult when it comes to marketing. That doesn't mean you shouldn't try. It makes sense to plan for it up front instead of trying to figure it out afterwards. Thinking through how you're going to get your ROI numbers before you start marketing is a good idea.

"An example might be a company with $100,000 in sales and a 40% gross margin that wants to increase their revenues by 10% and they're currently spending 3% of their total revenues on marketing."

Dave paused and looked at me. "Okay," I said to break the silence.

"How much can they invest in marketing?"

"How am I supposed to know that?" I asked.

He smiled and then looked over towards the infield. "If their starting revenues are $100,000 with a 40% gross margin that means the direct costs are $60,000, so at first base they'll have $40,000 left . . ."

"I get it! Then if the marketing increases their business by 10%, which is $10,000, they'll have $4,000 more of gross profit. If their additional marketing costs are less than $4,000 they'll get some ROI."

"That's right, except for one thing. The 40% gross margin already has 3% for marketing built in. So you also have to count 3% of the additional $10,000 in revenues, which is $300, and that makes total increase in gross profit $4,300. Now, you have to remember if you spend the whole $4,300 on marketing then you'll just be working harder for the same amount of profit. Not a good idea."

"Isn't that the supersize syndrome?" I asked.

"That's exactly what it looks like in action. Okay, back to the original question. I asked you how much they can invest in marketing. Now we know that answer. Next in line comes a more important question. How much should they invest in marketing?"

"That's a better question," I replied.

"Normally that's figured out in the forecasting stage of the forecast and variance report. The focus should be on improving the bottom line. As part of the process the owner needs to forecast the revenues and assign a marketing budget. To increase sales over the current run rate they'll likely have to invest more in their marketing and it sure would help to have some feedback to look at."

"I suppose that the better the marketing plan is, the lower the marketing budget needs to be. Wouldn't a good plan be more efficient at generating the revenues?"

"That's right. That's a big picture way of looking at the ROI of a whole Marketing Plan," said Dave. "It's also a very good practice to plan to measure the initiatives within the plan to see which ones are getting the best ROI. It's fairly easy to do with hunting and farming activities, but it's a bit tricky with fishing activities."

"Why's that?" I asked.

"Well, when you build a website or advertise in the newspaper, for example, it can be difficult to tell how much business you actually get from it—let alone gross profit. You can put in a coupon or monitor traffic on a special landing page but it's not always clear where the business comes from. If you're running a few initiatives at once even your customers might not be sure which one got their attention. Your front line employees are going to need good habits and a healthy curiosity to give you good feedback. You should be thinking about how you can help them with this, back when you're developing your marketing calendar."

"Got it."

"I've got another math problem for you. If you run a 20% off special on a product that sells for $100 and costs $60, then you support it with $400 in advertising, how many units do you have to sell to break even?"

"Okay, let's see. We started with a $40 gross profit and with the special it's now down to $20 of gross profit per unit. There's $400 in expenses to cover, so that makes twenty units."

"That's it, but again there's another catch. Out in the business world they have to consider the units they would have sold at the regular price during their normal course of business. Let's say they would have sold five at full price without the special. Then they should also make up for the five $20 discounts they gave to the customers who would have paid full price. Their true breakeven comes at twenty-five units."

"That's not fair Dave, you didn't tell me about that."

"I know Jen, no worries. I just wanted to make the point that a company can sell five units or twenty-five units and make the same amount of gross profit. It's interesting to know how the ROI works. Once you start seeing the ROI from your overall marketing and the ROI from the initiatives then you've got some good information and that in turn will improve your choices going forward. To get an accurate picture marketing ROI should always be calculated with gross profit dollars instead of revenues."

"That is an eye opener. Point made, you're forgiven Dave."

"It's well worth the effort to learn this and put the systems in place. When a company develops a good marketing plan that's generating a solid ROI, they can grow the business, when they want to, in a way that positively impacts their profitability. That's powerful stuff."

"No kidding. I've heard that over 50% of small company owners have indicated that they could use some training in marketing."

"One last thought before I sum up. When a company runs its marketing plan over an extended period of time a residual builds up. Customers remember it and some customers repeat. Done right the customers will keep coming for a while after the marketing is discontinued. There's also a way to do it wrong. If West Valley Auto consistently advertises cheap oil changes, to attract customers, then eventually it will get a reputation for that. They might lose out on potential clients who want a full service shop. That's another reason for the calendar. You can look at it and get a sense of what the overall impression will be."

"Alright, where's the big finish?"

"Here it is; I've kept you in suspense for long enough. We've talked about how the marketing plan should be the company's bridge to their chosen market. The six challenges are:

Benefits with buy-in
Resistance and risk
Initiating contact and exchanging information
Delivering value with your message
Getting feedback
Evaluating your ROI"

"That's right, I've got all that here in my notes, but I'm still waiting for the big finish."

Dave had another one of those huge grins on his face. I was wondering what I was missing.

After a minute he asked, "What are the first letters?"

I started to write them out. B, R, I, D, G, E, and then I started to chuckle. "You're kidding me!"

Dave laughed. "I'm starting to phase myself out of the day to day operations over at Velocity and it's given me a lot of time to think and improve on the marketing plan element. Anyways," he said as he took a deep breath, "the first two letters are the preparation challenges, the middle two are the delivery challenges, and the last two letters are the review challenges. It's the BRIDGE marketing plan."

"That's awesome."

"Sometimes the elements combine and this is a good example. A strong company promise is vital. The AR^2T of momentum is very effective at bringing a BRIDGE marketing plan to life. It could also be fifteen to twenty lines on the CA^3M. That depends on the company and how complex of a marketing plan they need."

"I can see that. Most of my clients have AR^2T forms going on their marketing now. When I show them this it will really accelerate the process and get them to their results much faster. But it's a lot to take in. We can use AR^2T forms to break it into manageable chunks." I smiled to myself because Karl Anders Ericsson often referred to chunking and I didn't fully grasp what he meant until now. Then I realized that Dave had chunked marketing into six challenges with his BRIDGE acronym. Everything seemed to be connecting.

"I think Jones will like it. If you can fit it into your presentation on Monday it should help."

"Thanks Dave, I really appreciate it. This is very interesting on a whole lot of levels."

Dave motioned to Nora for the bill and we walked up to the till.

"We should meet next Tuesday morning at ten in my office," he said. "I'd like to get the blow by blow account of your presentation to Jones. Stan tells me that it's pretty good and from what I've heard about it I think Jones will be impressed."

"I'll make Tuesday happen," I said. We filled the air with casual chatter as we left the Diamond and headed to our cars. The rain had stopped and the sun was shining. It was going to be a good afternoon.

34

I arrived at work at 8:00 AM on Monday. It was March 15th, the Ides of March. My plan was to start the day by going over the forecasts with Alice. We were going to have to meet at the reception desk for sure.

After talking it over we figured the forecasts could wait until eleven. By then she should have the revisions back from Garth and Martin. After that I could call them and go over the areas where we could put the AR^{2}T of momentum to work. The current run rates would be the assessments, the revisions to their forecasts would be the results they wanted, then we could get started realizing the available options and put a TRaction plan in place, even if all it involved for now was reaching out to others for their input.

While I was waiting I reviewed my notes from the research I'd done on Sunday regarding building efficacy. On a second pass through it became clear that measuring success by personal improvements instead of victories over others was important. Mark, Teru, and Dave must have known this when the developed the slogan 'Everybody Wins'. Come to think of it, this is also perfectly consistent with the approach of building **a company that does business in a market**. Building a strong company doesn't necessarily have to be about beating somebody else.

It also became clear that too many easy successes early on can often lead to efficacy crashes later on. People who expect quick results are easily discouraged when things become more complex and challenging. A reasonable degree of difficulty and overcoming some obstacles along the way is actually required. I guess that goes back to Teru's 83rd problem.

Exposure to other people who are more advanced is also a good way to build efficacy. Especially if the more advanced person is viewed as similar to ourselves. We get clues when we observe others who we believe are like us, we draw comparisons from them about our own abilities to learn, grow, and perform. It's the 'if she can, I can', type of idea.

I imagine that's why it's a good idea for company owners to participate in industry associations and business groups.

As I compared Bloom's work to Ericsson's work and I came up with some interesting observations. Ericsson's work was all about reaching the highest levels possible while Bloom's philosophy was; if you can teach something to someone, you can teach it to almost everyone—if you approach it the right way. That seems to be promising for company owners and their employees.

Both appeared to realize that well designed challenges and or deliberate practices were vital. Sustaining motivation was also crucial especially with Ericsson's subjects. The road to the very top is much longer and a lot tougher. There's only one winner of the gold medal at the end of the journey. Competition with others becomes inevitable.

I thought that was spot on. For example, not every company that writes software has to compete with Microsoft or needs to get that huge. Velocity Software was doing very well and Dave seemed to be having a great life.

I met with Alice at 11:00 AM and we went over the revisions that Grant and Martin had requested. Alice was going to make the changes on the forecast spreadsheets and I started the AR^{2}T forms. They were similar to the ones that we were already working with, but not the same. I e-mailed both of them to see when we could get together to discuss combining the two sets of forms. Alice said she would have the revisions done by the end of the day so I asked for appointments on Tuesday afternoon if possible.

The rest of the day flew past. I typed up the notes from Saturday's BRIDGE marketing meeting with Dave. There was a knock on my door. I looked at my watch and at was ten to three. I put my presentation materials together and headed down to Mr. Jones' office.

35

I found myself sitting in my Honda Civic out in front of the old coffee shop. I didn't even remember driving there.

All I remember is Mr. Jones telling me that my services were no longer required. I didn't get to do my presentation.

He said that I wasn't billing out any hours and it didn't appear that I was anywhere near finished the whitepaper. I tried to tell him that I'd only had ten weeks so far and I was starting to make good progress.

He glared at me over his glasses and said that I was even dragging other people into it with me and the firm couldn't afford that. I knew that he meant Alice.

When I got back to my office I found someone in there already packing my personal effects into a box. I was handed my final pay and given the box.

As I walked through the reception area Alice was coming out of the conference room with the office manager right behind her. She said they found out that she was working on the forecasts again this morning and she had just been given her two weeks' notice. The office manager stood and watched me leave.

My brain was locked up and I could hardly think. I got out of the car and headed towards the coffee shop because I didn't know what else to do. Even walking was an effort. Every step I had to consciously think about moving my feet. It felt like if my feet stopped I'd just sit down on the sidewalk and cry.

Getting fired was bad enough, but taking Alice down with me was more than I could bear.

"Jen, my god, what happened?" Haley called out as she rushed from behind the counter. "Are you all right? Here, have a seat."

I didn't remember crying but I guess my mascara was streaked down my cheeks. I must have looked pretty bad for her to react like that.

"I got fired."

"What for?" she asked.

"I don't know."

"What?"

"He wasn't happy with my progress on the paper or that Alice was helping me with it."

"That's bullcrap, he's a real jerk. He shouldn't fire somebody like that especially when you had to quit your job here to go over and work for him. Unless you screwed up and he's the one who screwed up. Stan was telling me that you weren't getting anywhere near the level of support you needed."

"That's not the worst part," I said. "Alice got fired too."

Haley looked at me incredulously. "You have to be kidding me! How does that guy stay in business?"

"I don't know what to think," I said.

"Well I do, wait here. I'll get you a coffee on me."

It took her longer that it should have. When she came back she started talking right away. "Stan's coming right over," was the first thing she said and I didn't really hear the rest.

When Stan got there we sat and talked for a while. I don't remember too much about what was said but I do remember that he kept saying that he had a lot of respect for me and how he didn't think that Mr. Jones kept up his end of the bargain and provide the support and feedback I needed to be successful. Stan believed that I was thrown into the deep end without a life preserver.

He also recounted the story of how Dave hired him when he was pretty green and he brought him along.

Haley invited us both to go out for dinner and bowling afterwards to get my mind off of it.

It was hard to stop thinking about it. When we were at the bowling alley I tried to call Alice a couple of times to talk, but she didn't answer her phone or return my messages.

When I got back to my apartment I couldn't shut my mind off and go to sleep so I watched old movies until 4:20 AM then went to bed drifting in and out of sleep until the phone rang at 10:15 AM

36

I reached over and picked up the phone. It was Stan. "Jen, where are you?"

"I'm at home sleeping in because I don't have a job anymore," I answered.

"What about your 10:00 AM meeting with Dave?" he asked.

"Oh crap, I forgot about that," I said. "But it doesn't matter anymore because the project is over now."

"I've got news for you. Yesterday wasn't the end. It was the start of a new beginning."

"What?" I was confused.

"There is absolutely no way that Dave is going to tell Mark that the project is over. This thing is going full speed ahead come hell or high water."

"You're kidding me. I better get up and down there right away," I said as I jumped out of bed and scrambled around to get dressed. "Tell Dave I'll be there in twenty minutes."

"You can take your time now. Dave's gone over to Carey Jones Norton to meet with Mr. Jones. He wants to get the rights to the project and more specifically to have Jones sign off on it so he can't come back on him. I don't know if Jones was more afraid to take the meeting or avoid it. Dave was pretty ramped up when he called. He was talking about having everybody he knew pull their business from Carey Jones Norton if he didn't get ushered into Jones' office as soon as he arrived. I don't remember ever seeing Dave that upset before."

"I wish that I could be a fly on the wall for that meeting," I said.

"I took me a few minutes to calm him down. I think that he's better now; he really has his mind set on seeing this project through. He was telling me a story about something Mark said to him a few months back. Mark told him that he didn't care what anybody said at his funeral. That exercise is promoted by self-help gurus and it's basically just a waste of time. You're dead and can't hear anyways. Mark told him what really matters is that when you take your last breath you should know that you made a difference in this world. If you've made your life a gift to the world, death is easier to accept. Then apparently Mark added: 'The only thing I really want to hear people saying at my funeral is: hey, look he's moving!'"

We both laughed. After a bit Stan carried on. "Before he left Dave was talking about making certain that Mark knew he gave a really big gift with his life. Then he mumbled something about this project originally being his and Mark's idea anyways and somehow Jones got a hold of it. He wrote you a note before he left."

I rushed down to Velocity Software. I wanted to be there when Dave got back. As I walked through the front door the receptionist Iola said, "It's nice to see you this morning, Miss Russell, or do you prefer Ms?"

"Jen is fine," I replied.

"Jen it is then. Can you follow me down to your office please?"

"What's that?" I asked, shocked by the question.

"It's furnished a little sparsely but I think you'll find it comfortable enough," she replied.

We walked past the meeting room and down the hall. Just before we turned to the right into the bullpen she pointed down the hall and said, "The lunch room and Mr. Ettinger's office are further down that way, but I'm sure you know that."

As we made small talk while we were walking through the bullpen I looked over towards Stan's desk with the straw umbrella. He wasn't there. My new office was one of the four at the far end. Iola walked me to the door before she left to go back to her reception desk.

I went around my new desk and sat down in the comfortable high-backed chair. The office was bare except for a faded old newspaper article that was framed and hung on the wall. There was a note taped to the bottom of the frame. I got up and went over to take a look at it. There was a picture of a young softball coach kneeling down to tape up a player's running shoe. The sole was coming apart from the runner.

I started to read the article and discovered that Mark was the coach and the player was Teru. The article described how a brand new young coach, Mark, had taken over the team when his boss from work, the original coach, was transferred out of town on short notice. It turned out that the team was having a Cinderella season. Against all odds they made it all the way to the regional finals. It was a seven game series for the championship. Mark and Teru's team won the first three games, but then unfortunately they had to forfeit their three wins to the opposing team. The player in the picture, Teru, had played two games for another team at the start of the season. The proper paperwork for a transfer hadn't been filed with the association.

Then I read the note. It was from Dave to me. Their team eventually lost the series in game seven. Mark didn't know Teru had played for another team earlier in the year. He wouldn't have known how to file the transfer paperwork anyways. He was a first time coach and he was only twenty years old at the time.

It all happened because Teru was always hanging around the ballpark when Mark's team was practicing. One day Mark just asked him if he wanted to play.

Apparently Teru had quit his original team because the coaches and players on the team teased him mercilessly about being Japanese. World War Two had just ended a few years before.

Mark will never forget the day he had to sit in front of the league's commissioners and try to explain his side of the story to them. There was no mercy shown at all; they enforced the rules as written. He asked if they would consider forfeiting only one game because the opposing coaches apparently knew about the technicality all along and they didn't speak up about it. The commissioners didn't even respond. They acted as if he hadn't spoken at all.

The next year Mark started a league in West Valley. They didn't enter a team into the districts or regional championships for almost ten years. Finally Teru started coaching too and told Mark to get over it.

Later on baseball became more popular with boys. West Valley ran teams for both baseball and softball for a while. Some of the baseball parents didn't get the 'Everybody Wins' philosophy and moved their kids over to a different league. Then Mark and Teru started some girls' softball teams. Eventually boys' softball died right off and there was only the West Valley girls' league left.

I went back to my new desk and sat down. I knew the project was finally where it belonged.

Epilogue

It was Saturday, April 14th, a bright sunny spring day, a little over a year after Dave got control of the project when I invited Alice and Haley to meet me for lunch at the Diamond. I had some big news. Stan and I were getting married in August and I was about to ask them if they would be my bridesmaids.

I'd taken the time to get to know Nora Chang and tell her about the Company Strength Program. She in turn explained it to her parents and they were implementing the concepts. The Diamond is coming back around. I'd chosen to make this my gift to Dave, Teru and Mark. They would have done it themselves years ago, but they couldn't figure out how to communicate effectively with the Changs.

Haley doesn't work at the coffee shop anymore she's finally gotten her dream job working at a graphic design firm. Alice was amazingly still working at Carey Jones Norton. Dave spoke very highly of her when he was chewing out Mr. Jones. CJN wound up rehiring her and giving her a promotion. I guess he's not that bad after all. She's now working full time with one of the firm's lead accountants. He's a great mentor for Alice. She's really enjoying her work now and is learning fast.

Stan was chosen as the new CEO for Velocity Software. They're working their way through the succession plan. January fourth of next year is the official handover date. Dave cautioned the new ownership group that while they might own the company they'll never really own the business because Velocity Software doesn't have a monopoly. The best they can do is to secure the business by consistently keeping the company promise.

The company accountability matrix (CA³M) was very effective for shifting Dave's accountabilities and responsibilities over to Stan in an orderly fashion. Stan in turn cascaded his down into the organization. Everyone who wanted to advance within the company was given the opportunity to move up. At the end of the process they'll need to add a junior employee. Dave is taking some kidding about being replaced by a stock boy, but he appears to be taking all it all in good sport. I think.

Dave put his retirement on hold so he and I could start a new company: ROCK SOLID Company Strength. We secured the web address: www. company-strength.com. Dave let me know that he wants to be out of the day to day operations as soon as he can. We are using the five key elements to strengthen our new company as fast as realistically possible. Our company promise is, 'delivering business success by using a straightforward approach that strengthens companies.' We designed a visual to represent the five elements of the company strength program.

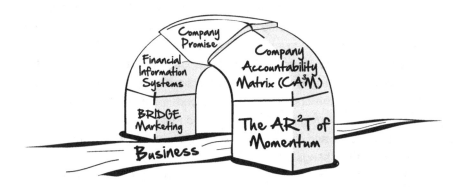

ROCK SOLID has taken on eight new clients, mostly through referrals from my clients and the Breakfast Boys. We haven't done much marketing up to this point, mostly because the referrals have kept us busy. We're laying the groundwork to expand into other markets. We plan to find and train licensed Company Strength Specialists and increase the program's geographical coverage. Having a complete BRIDGE marketing plan prepared for the licensed Company Strength Specialists is important. I'm excited about the future.

Somehow Dave also managed to negotiate a deal with Mr. Jones where Alice could do some work for ROCK SOLID's clients. It's mostly preparing forecast and variance reports. I've really been enjoying working with her even though we're at different companies now.

I understand how critical these F & V reports are. If a company is profitable it can stay in the game and think through how and when a deliberate practice plan for building a strong company can be implemented. Profits are, without a doubt, the best fuel for growth. Setting up a business model to consistently get around third and score runs is challenging for a lot of companies. The F & V Reports are an awesome learning tool in this respect. They provide great feedback.

All my clients are doing well, even Ron from Waltham Signs. Dave helped him work out his company promise: 'we bring customers inside'. It's opened up a whole new way of thinking and selling for Ron. It's not about the product anymore. His enthusiasm has even spilled over to his clients. Ron's talking to everybody in town about how they get new customers. Location is often a big part of that, so the creative use signage becomes very important. We've got his forecast and variance reporting set up. We're using the CA³M to systemize his operations and he's been using the AR²T of momentum religiously. His five year plan is to double his business while maintaining a ten percent bottom line. I think that will be challenging, but he's working hard on his BRIDGE marketing plan.

Ben from ABC Landscaping has his third crew working, he's been very happy with the quality of their work. He's only on the tools himself for about fifteen hours a week now and the company is rounding third and scoring runs. His company promise is, 'manicured like my Mom is coming to inspect it'. Everybody gets a chuckle from that, except his Mom. We've got a CA³M finished, complete with all his systems and the forecast & variance reports are up and running as well. ABC is exceeding their forecasted profits almost every month. They're active with the AR²T of momentum and we're continuing to refine his BRIDGE marketing plan. His five year plan has the company expanding into the next town over with Ben transitioning to 100% owner manager.

Martin can't believe how well Hydro Plumbing is running. He credits the CA³M for the improvements on the operational side. Everyone now knows what they're accountable and responsible for. He credits the forecast and variance reports for his improved profitability. The KPIs are big for him too. He's on the program with the AR²T of momentum and his company promise is, 'done properly, on time, on budget, by the best tradespeople you'll ever work with'. It's a big promise and keeping it has led to a lot of changes at Hydro Plumbing. As for the marketing plan, he chose to stay the same size once he realized that he didn't have to grow to be profitable. His five year plan is to save his profits for a down payment and then buy his own building.

Grant from West Valley Auto really dialled on his BRIDGE marketing plan. That was the key for him to reach his car count and productivity ratio goals. Some of the best marketing ideas involved farming his existing client base. Once they understand how maintenance extends the life of their vehicles and how they can save a huge amount of money by keeping their vehicles for an extra three of four years his clients more readily give their go ahead to the mechanics' recommendations. BRIDGE marketing and the AR²T of momentum are working well together. The recreational vehicle client base is now up to fifty seven and growing steadily. He expects to hit his goal of one hundred by the spring of next year. Alice does his forecast and variance reports and the company is reaching his profit targets consistently now, although he still has challenges hitting his productivity KPIs some months. His company promise is now, 'hometown service, knowledgeable technicians helping you get the most out of your vehicle'. In five years he wants to have the company running well enough that he can start a photography company.

Ray over at the St. John Pub got his costs under control using the forecast and variance reports and he used the CA³M matrix to systemize his whole organization. Establishing accountabilities, responsibilities, and clear lines of communication was very effective at getting his kitchen to run the way he wanted it to. His company promise was simple: 'a fun and friendly pub with great food'. Everything is aimed directly at that. They're also using curiosity well. The BRIDGE marketing plan is using a lot of different tactics for initiating contact and it's increased the guest count. We're continuing to work on it, that AR²T form on that is still open and it may be for a while yet. The good news is that he's consistently around third, although scoring runs is challenging in the winter months. The recent change in traffic patterns that diverted traffic off his street over onto a newly built arterial road is still having an impact on his sales. Within five years Ray would like to add another location.

In our new clients' companies the CA³M was proving to be great for the other important commodity that company owners are all too often short of: time. The CA³M coordinates the systemization of companies and that saves everyone time. When the company's functions are all inventoried on the CA³M with accountabilities, responsibilities and communications delegated out effectively—the owners have more time—for designing, building and managing their companies. It's clearly a great tool for escaping from the Valley of the Lost Entrepreneurs.

The CA³M process closely resembles the Holmes complexity quotation in a lot of ways. At first it can take a bit to wrap your mind around it, but then it provides the most straightforward route to building a strong company that's ever been developed.

It also follows Ericsson's theory on high performance. It details everything that happens in a company. It becomes, in effect an inventory of all the functions, or tasks if you will, that are involved in the ongoing operation of the company. To make it easier to follow they should be divided into sub-sections like: accounting, administration, operations, sales, marketing, and meetings for example. The sub-sections should make sense for the company.

It even pays to include functions that aren't happening yet, but will strengthen the company when they're added. This puts them on the radar for implementation at the appropriate time. An example of this might be a BRIDGE marketing plan. A company should get their operations running well before they add a lot of new customers into the mix. In that case you might put the marketing functions onto the CA³M with no accountabilities, responsibilities or systems yet. The marketing functions then become deliberate practice sessions to be scheduled in at a later date.

The functions are down the first column, on the vertical axis, of a spreadsheet and the people are listed across the top row, on the horizontal axis. We build the CA³Ms on Excel spreadsheets.

Then the letters **A, R, M, C, I & b** are distributed.

A is the most critical letter. The reason that it's cubed with the little three over top is because it stands for **a**nswerable, **a**uthority, and **a**ttention. Every function must have an **A**. The person with the **A** is **a**nswerable for that function, has **a**uthority to make changes and must pay **a**ttention to the way it's performing. I didn't know, is clearly not a valid excuse.

R stands for **r**esponsibility and is assigned to the people who actually perform the function. The person assigned the **A** is tasked with ensuring the people with the **R**s are response-able and can perform the functions well.

The lower case **b** stands for backup, which could be holiday relief.

When you have somebody who's accountable, somebody who's responsible, a documented system in place, and a trained backup then you've got real company strength. That's the end game for the CA³M process. I'm finding out that it's not rocket science. It's just a series of steps that any company can work through. Its Bloom's theory—if you can teach something to somebody, then it's possible to teach it to almost anybody. It just takes time, but the end result is well worth the effort.

The **M** stands for meeting. The meetings that the company holds, or should hold. They are listed in their own sub-section in the first column and the **M**s are assigned to people who should be at those meetings. Note: the duties of the meetings are also listed as functions. For example: scheduling, agenda preparation & distribution, room prep, facilitator/chair, minute taker, and minute distribution are all standard functions.

A side note: most of the world's prominent business icons spend a large percentage of their time in meetings. It's reasonable to assume there is a cause-effect relationship there. The reason that most small company owners don't like meetings is because they haven't been to many good ones yet. Getting good at holding and attending meetings is virtually guaranteed to improve almost any company. This is another example of getting results from taking several swings on the gate with a deliberate practice approach.

The next two letters involve other forms of communication. I stands for inform and that letter is assigned to the people who need to be informed about the happenings in the function. The **C** is assigned to people who need to be consulted before the activities in the function take place.

The difference between the **I** and the **C** is the timing of the communication. The **I** stands for informing afterwards and the **C** is for consulting beforehand. The communication can take many forms. For example, a text, phone call, e-mail, memo, informal face to face, specifically designed report, or whatever other means that is agreed to in advance and approved by the person with the **A**.

Functions	Current Strength	Frequency	Documented	Owner	Sales Manager	Sales Reps
SALES						
Sales Presentations					AI	R
Quotations under $10,000					AI	R
Quotations over $10,000					AC	R
Weekly Sales Meetings				M	ARM	M
Weekly Sales Reports				I	AR	I
Sales Forecasts				AC	R	IC

A couple of examples will bring this to life. Imagine a company with four sales reps and a sales manager. The sales manager will have the **A** for the sales presentations function because he or she is ultimately answerable for the results. The position also holds the authority when it comes to making choices and decisions regarding the function. The person in this role also has to pay attention, which means he or she has to regularly think through all aspects of the presentations and ensure that the systems and processes are well designed and delivering the desired results. Once again, it also means that 'I didn't know' is simply not a valid excuse. One **A** and only one **A** must be assigned for every function the company performs.

The sales reps will be assigned an **R** because they are the people who are actually out in the field performing the function of delivering the sales presentations. It's their responsibility to deliver a certain amount of presentations of a predetermined quality and to close a certain percentage. The sales manager with the **A** must ensure that the sales reps assigned with the **R** are response-able and consistently perform to the standards of the company.

In this example the sales manager would also have an **I**. They need to be informed of the happenings in the field. In most cases that would be a daily or weekly report that's specifically designed for the purpose.

I can also imagine that there would be a second very similar function line where the sales manager would have a **C** instead of an **I**. This might be for quotes over $10,000. It makes sense that larger quotes should be run past the sales manager before they are delivered to the prospect.

Functions	Current Strength	Frequency	Documented	Owner	Accountant	A/P Clerk
ACCOUNTS PAYABLE						
Enter Invoices with Purchase Orders					AI	R
Enter Invoices over $500.00 without Purchase Orders					AC	R
Reconcile Supplier Accounts					I	AR
Accounts Payable Problem Solving				I	AR	C
Produce Aged Payables Report				I	I	AR

Another good example is the entry of accounts payable invoices into the accounting system. In this case the company's own internal accountant would be assigned the **A** because they are ultimately answerable for the integrity of the books. An Accounts Payable Clerk may be assigned entry function and given the **R**. Again there may be two very similar function lines one for invoices with purchase orders and a second function line for invoices over $500 without purchase orders. In the first case the accountant would have an **I** while in the second they would have a **C**. The communication around the **C** would likely be a file folder for pending authorizations and or a face to face discussion if there are further clarifications required.

A couple of things are challenging when you first start implementing the CA³M. A lot of people initially aren't certain about the distinction between **A**ccountability and **R**esponsibility but the difference is pretty clear. Many people tend to overuse the word responsibility, the buck stops at the **A**. If there is a problem the person who is **A**ccountable has to ensure that it gets sorted out. They're also in charge of authorizing and improving the underlying systems, procedures, and policies. The person assigned an **R** is response-able. They are the doer. Their role is to follow the company's systems, procedures, and policies while performing their functions to the best of their abilities. They should also be expected to suggest improvements and assist with the creation of documented systems if required.

I strongly believe in the advice from Dave's wife Karen: always leave it cleaner than you found it. This translates to: if you work at a company always plan to leave it stronger than when you started there. As an owner you have to wonder how long you want to keep someone in your company who doesn't have this attitude.

A person who's assigned an **R** shouldn't wash their hands of system, policy, and procedure development. Having open and frank discussions in this area is critical to improving the strength of, and ongoing performance of the company. In my mind these discussions are a function in their own right and it should be listed on the CA³M. Most companies don't put enough time into this, but those that do are basically insuring their future success. There's a fascinating example in the story below.

It's interesting to think about the standard QWERTY keyboards that virtually every computer has today. They were named after the keys in the top row of letters starting from the left. QWERTY keyboards were originally engineered with two design parameters in mind. First, to slow typists down. Yes this is sad, but true. The keyboard layout that everybody uses today was deliberately designed to work against us.

The QWERTY keyboard was engineered back in the old typewriter days when the typist pushed a key down and a lever swung the corresponding letter up towards a moving ribbon with ink on it. The resulting impact transferred the ink onto the page in the shape of the letter. The apparatus had to be manually shifted back to left at the end of each and every line.

A fast typist could easily jam more than one lever in the slot at the same time so the QWERTY keyboard layout was designed to help prevent this from happening. The second design feature of the QWERTY was to have all of the letters in TYPEWRITER in the top row because the sales reps that were out selling typewriters (who couldn't type) could then easily utilize a two finger approach when typing the word typewriter to impress their prospects.

Why are we still using these keyboards today? It just doesn't make any sense at all.

We all get caught up doing strange things, like using the standard QWERTY keyboard, without thinking about it, mostly because that's the way we've always done it. The process of developing a company accountability matrix examines the way everything is done in your company and it will naturally identify any 'QWERTYs' that you have hiding in your organization.

In an interesting twist, CA³M meetings should also be listed in the meeting section of the CA³M. This is another function that benefits from multiple swings on the gate. The frequency of the CA³M meetings should be higher at the beginning of the process and then taper off as it comes together. The initial implementation can take forty to fifty hours to reach critical mass but the work can and should be split up amongst several people.

The second thing that's challenging about the CA³M is most people don't realize how many moving parts there are in their company and how often they move. The inventory of functions will wind up being a fair bit longer than you think going in. A company with a $1,000,000 in revenues could be as long as six pages when it's printed out.

For more insight, let's revisit the sales example. The presentations that we mentioned earlier are only one part of the process. It could easily involve generating lists of prospects, researching prospects, getting the decision maker's contact information, answering incoming inquiries, website development, social media, the scripting and sending of direct mail pieces and e-mails, outbound phone calls, scheduling presentation appointments, quote preparation, follow up calls, opening accounts, and preparing order sheets. That's thirteen functions. Not to mention that all of that is based on having marketing in place.

When you add in the rest of the functions from bookkeeping, accounting, admin, human resources, management processes, production systems, daily openings and closings, et cetera, most companies have a pretty impressive inventory of moving parts that should be listed on their CA³M.

You might think that it's a lot of work to list the company's functions and perhaps even wonder about the wisdom of including everything on the CA³M but the next steps are revealing.

The second column is titled Current Strength. This is where we ask the owner, management team and most importantly the person with the **A** to be honest about how well each function is performing. In the diagram below we use the same A, B, C, letter grade scale that most people are familiar with from their school days. When the CA³M is completed the Current Strength column should be reviewed at regular intervals to identify where improvements are being made. It's very effective for developing employee performance plans.

We use the third column for frequency. That's the number of times that function is performed by the company in a year. Just like doing a physical inventory, the amount is calculated. In this process they will be mostly estimations. An organization might prepare 600 quotes under $10,000 every year. They would list the function in first column and 600 would be entered as the frequency in the second column. It's recommended to forecast the frequency expected for the upcoming year as opposed to calculating the amount from last year. The amounts of presentations and quotes aren't equal because not every presentation turns into a quote.

Functions	Current Strength	Frequency	Documented	Owner	Sales Manager	Sales Reps
SALES						
Sales Presentations	B+	900	SSH-2		AI	R
Quotations under $10,000	A	600	SSH-3		AI	R
Quotations over $10,000	B	100	SSH-4		AC	R
Weekly Sales Meetings	C+	52	PM-7.3	M	ARM	M
Weekly Sales Reports	A	52	PM-8	I	AR	I
Annual Sales Forecasts	B	1	PM-12	AC	R	IC

The next column is titled Documented. Here is where it's noted if there's a documented system, procedure, or policy in place. We like to have the notation indicate where it can be found. SSH-3 might indicate that it's found in the Sales Systems Handbook on page 3 for example or PM-7.3 might indicate that it's in the Policy Manual—Section 7, Paragraph 3. Every company has their own methods of cataloging their policies and systems.

If there currently isn't a system, procedure, or policy in place then we put 'need' in the documented column. Note: there are some functions that don't need anything and those are left blank. Guess who is in charge of getting the needed system, procedure of police written? It's the person with the A. They can, of course, delegate. Often it's the person with the R who is best able to write the system and we've made it fairly easy to do with our templates. Sometimes it's more efficient to bring in somebody from the outside. At ROCK SOLID we provide that service. At the end of the day though, the person with the A has to review the systems and authorize them. It can take two or three drafts, but if you have the A you might just be surprised how much you learn about what really happens in your department as you go through this process.

A series of meetings, the function column and the documented column combine with the templates to become a system for systemizing any company. In my initial research I often heard that systemizing a business was a great thing to do, but somewhat ironically I didn't see a system for systemizing until I was introduced to the CA³M. After a few swings on the gate I've come to realize how powerful it is.

When it's filled out the CA³M becomes a remarkable document for developing deliberate practice plans for companies that want to achieve high performance. Our clients who've built CA³Ms have found that they're miles ahead of where they used to be. The CA³M gives them a more powerful perspective and puts them in a much better position to plan for the future. It's also considerably easier for them to delegate effectively.

It's important to note that the CA³M, forecast and variance report, BRIDGE marketing plan and AR²T forms and are all living and breathing documents. They should be regularly reviewed and updated.

It may seem to be a lot of work to get a CA³M set up. Like everything else it takes time to implement and absorb. Remember from Ericsson's work that deliberate practice is not inherently enjoyable but if you really want to reach high levels of performance this has proven to be the only road available and the rewards are amazing.

We are discovering that when company owners do the work and integrate the five key elements they gain far more than they invest. Owners who decide not to strengthen their companies because they're too busy doing business always wind up paying a steeper price in the long run. They suffer from symptoms that can include: lower than needed revenues, tight cash flow, low or no profits, frustrations caused by staff not taking responsibility, endless problems, continuous customer service issues, and the owners themselves putting in long hours because the company is dependent on them. This is what Dave calls getting stuck in the Valley of the Lost Entrepreneurs.

Entrepreneurs bring business ideas to life while company owners build profitable organizations. It involves a shifting of mindsets. It's not 100% one way or the other, but at some point the entrepreneur mindset has to move over to make room for the company owner mindset or the enterprise won't develop to its full potential.

When a company isn't strong enough to handle the amount of business that it's attempting to process the owner can easily get swept down into the

Valley of the Lost Entrepreneurs by an avalanche of symptoms. Implementing the five key elements avoids a trip to the valley. They're also proving to be the shortest route out of the valley. The five key elements focus owners on building strong companies that add value to their lives and to the lives of their clients.

Hey, look at the clock. It's time for me to head to the Diamond and have lunch with Haley and Alice. After that I just have to drop off the deposit for the hall and I'll have the rest of the afternoon to myself.

www.company-strength.com

.